Who the Hell is Carl Jung?

Who the hell is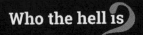

For students, teachers and curious minds, our **carefully structured jargon-free series** helps you really get to grips with brilliant intellectuals and their inherently complex theories.

Written in an **accessible and engaging** way, each book takes you through the **life and influences** of these brilliant intellectuals, before taking a deep dive into three of their **key theories in plain English**.

Smart thinking made easy!

POLITICS   PSYCHOLOGY   PHILOSOPHY   SOCIOLOGY   ART HISTORY

Who the Hell is Carl Jung?

And what are his theories all about?

Sarah Milne

**BOWDEN
&BRAZIL**

First published in Great Britain in 2023 by
Bowden & Brazil Ltd
Felixstowe, Suffolk, UK.

British Library Cataloguing-in-Publication Data
A CIP record for this book is available from The British Library.

Academic advisor: Dr Stuart Lipscombe, University of Suffolk, UK.

ISBN 978-1-915177-09-4

To find out more about other books and authors in this series,
visit www.whothehellis.co.uk

Contents

Introduction   1

1. Carl Jung's Life Story   5

2. Influences on Carl Jung's Thinking   33

3. The Human Psyche and Personality   51

4. The Personal and Collective Unconsciouses   71

5. Inner Work, Dreams and Therapy   89

Conclusion   103

Bibliography   109

Introduction

Carl Gustav Jung (1875–1961) is among psychology's biggest pioneers and one of the most important thinkers of the 20th century. He was a polymath with an avid interest in psychology, psychiatry, medicine, mythology, religion, philosophy, astronomy and alchemy, drawing all these together in his deep understanding of the human mind. This enabled him to create a bridge between our conscious and unconscious, shedding light on our interaction with the world.

Jung's understanding of humanity grew directly from understanding himself. He was a genius at introspection, the observation of his inner thoughts and feelings, and his theories evolved from meticulous study of his own mind. Jung's innermost experiences came from a time of 'creative illness' between 1913 and 1916, during which he conducted daily explorations and experiments into his own unconscious. These experiences were pivotal for Jung and formed the basis and scientific principles behind his theoretical framework of the human psyche and personality. During this time, he created a calligraphic illuminated manuscript from his journals and mandala art which would later become *Liber Novus* (*New Book*) commonly known as *The Red Book* (2009).

Fig. 1 *The Red Book* (Liber Novus) by C.G. Jung, resting on Jung's office desk.

The Red Book depicts Jung's voyage of discovery into his deepest self through part journal of his inner work and realizations about his own mind and the human psyche, and part mythological novel based on his self-induced controlled hallucinations as he journeyed to the deepest, inner core of his unconscious (see Chapter 5 for more on Jung's process of 'active imagination'). Jung commissioned a bookbinder to make an enormous volume of pages covered in red leather into which he poured his self-explorations, depicted in ornate calligraphy and psychedelic paintings of the mythical characters he found in his dreams and waking fantasies. In one section, Jung tells a story that begins:

> *'I find that I am standing on the highest tower of a*
> *castle. The air tells me so: I am far back in time. My gaze*
> *wanders widely over solitary countryside, a combination*

of fields and forests. I am wearing a green garment. A horn hangs from my shoulder. I am the tower guard. I look out into the distance. I see a red point out there. It comes nearer on a winding road…it is a horseman in a red coat, the red horseman… he knocks: a strange fear comes over me: there stands the red one… I think: in the end he will turn out to be the devil.' (Jung, 2009)

While the theories Jung developed through his inner work gained popularity, he feared the fantastical and unconventional words and images written in his red book could damage his acceptance and reputation in the scientific and psychological community of his time. He wrote in the opening of his journal that 'to the superficial observer' the contents would 'appear like madness' (Jung, 2009) and, throughout his life time, very few of his closest followers and colleagues were permitted to look inside the mysterious, red book that sat in his office.

Finally, after many years of persuasion by scholars and followers, the Jung family agreed to let the world peer inside *The Red Book*, and it was finally published in 2009, 48 years after Jung's death. This led to a surge of interest in Jung among intellectuals, psychologists, spiritual and religious thinkers, artists, writers, filmmakers and creators across the world, making him one of the most influential minds of the 21st century.

Who the Hell is Carl Jung? explores Jung's life and inspirations, the influences that impacted his thinking, and the key theories that he has brought to the world of psychology. The third and fourth chapters look at his main theories of the human psyche and personality, and his understanding of the unconscious and archetypes. However, Jung's psychology was more than mere theory – it was a method; a process of self-discovery and transformation into the best version of ourselves; a way to fulfil our purpose and destiny. The final chapter therefore explores Jung's practical ideas and methods of 'inner work' and therapy. Finally, the book closes with some suggestions about Jung's importance and relevance to modern 21st-century life.

Jung was a prolific writer, though confessed, 'I have such a hell of a trouble to make people see what I mean' (1963). This book aims to explain his work in a way that is easily understandable and, we hope, inspirational for anyone new to his ideas.

1. Jung's Life Story

Carl Gustav Jung was born on 26 July 1875 in Keswill, a village on the Swiss banks of Lake Constance. When he was six years old, the family moved to Laufen, near the Falls of the Rhine, where his father, the Reverend Paul Achilles Jung (1842–1896), took up the post as the village protestant priest. Carl was the only surviving son of the Reverend and his wife, Emilie Preiswerk (1848–1923). Emily experienced two stillbirths before giving birth, in 1873, to Paul, named after his father. Sadly Paul lived only a few days. Carl's sister, Johanna Gertrud, was not born until 1884 and his nine years as an only child contributed greatly to the isolation and loneliness that plagued his early years, driving him to spend most of his time living in his inner mind. These 'inner experiences' formed his games as a child and became the origins of his later psychological ideas and practices.

Carl's parents were important influences in his childhood thinking and adult theorizing. His father was the son of Carl Gustav Jung (1794–1864), an esteemed physician and priest and after whom Carl was named. Emilie Jung was the youngest daughter of a well-known but eccentric pastor in Basel, Samuel Preiswerk (1799–1871); a Zionist who had visions and conversed with the dead. The Preiswerks were a large family consisting of many clergymen sharing Samuel's fascination with the occult. Carl's intellectual development was very much influenced by this mix of medicine, theology and spiritualism, which we will look at further in following chapter.

Emilie Jung's Illness and Maternal Separation

Alongside providing an interesting spiritual heritage, Carl's parents influenced their young son in other, more disturbing ways. Throughout his childhood, he was haunted by an atmosphere of melancholy, unease and, 'dim intimations of trouble,' in his parents' marriage (Jung, 1963). In 1878, when he was three years old, Emilie's unhappiness escalated into a psychiatric breakdown and she spent many months away in a psychiatric hospital. Carl was deeply troubled by this separation, experiencing nervous eczema and terrifying dreams. He wrote,

> *'From then on, I always felt mistrustful when the word "love" was spoken. The feeling I associated with "woman" was, for a long time, that of innate unreliability. "Father," on the other hand, meant reliability – and powerlessness.'* (1963)

To outsiders, the Reverend Jung was a compassionate and tolerant man. However, he had lost his faith early in his ministry and, with no other trade to fall back on, was compelled to continue with his work as a parish priest. The strain of keeping up appearances while lacking any religious conviction turned him into a cantankerous hypochondriac at home and someone his wife and son struggled to love and respect. Jung describes how,

'There arose in me profound doubts about everything my
father said. When I heard him preaching about grace,
I always thought of my own experience. What he said
sounded stale and hollow, like a tale told by someone
who knows it only by hearsay and cannot quite believe
it himself.' (Jung, 1963)

While his mother was in hospital, Carl was cared for by a spinster aunt, 20 years older than Emilie, along with the family maid. He was fascinated by this younger woman and felt a strange familiarity with her, a feeling of, 'having known her always' (Jung, 1963). This mysterious, deep connection with his maid later contributed to Jung's theory of 'anima', the idea of a feminine image and influence within men, and 'animus', the masculine within women (see Chapter 3). The maid, and the feelings she conveyed in the young boy, became central components of Jung's own anima, symbolizing for him the complete essence of womanhood.

Jung's First 'Big Dream'

The Laufen vicarage was a frightening place for Carl. The constant roar of the Rhine Falls, where many had been drowned, together with the nearby cemetery, gave him a feeling of being surrounded by danger. To help comfort him from his night fears, Emilie taught Carl a prayer: 'Spread out thy wings, Lord Jesus mild. And take to thee thy chick, thy child...' (Jung, 1963). Unfortunately, the prayer had the opposite effect and Carl's ruminative mind led him to form a sinister analogy of Jesus kidnapping children against their will, taking them in the ground and eating them to prevent Satan from eating them himself. He

Fig. 2 Jung's childhood home in Kleinhüningen, Basel, Switzerland.

began to distrust Jesus to the point that just hearing the name would traumatize him. One day, he overheard his father having a conversation about Jesuits. Though he didn't know what a 'Jesuit' was, the word sounded very much like Jesus. Days later, Carl was out playing and saw (as he later learned) a Catholic priest approaching. Believing this black figure to be a Jesuit, Carl hid for days in the house in, 'hellish fright' (Jung, 1963).

When he was three years old, Carl had the first dream he can remember. The emotion and symbolism held in this 'big dream' was to preoccupy his mind for the rest of his life. He was in the meadow, near the vicarage in Laufen, when he saw a large, dark hole that he had never seen before. Despite fear, Jung's curiosity led him to descend a dark staircase to the bottom, where he found a curtain hanging over an archway. On the other side was a long room with a magnificent throne at the end. On the throne sat a huge 'thing', around two feet wide, reaching almost to the ceiling. It looked like a tree-trunk but was made of naked skin and flesh. On top of the trunk was something that looked like a rounded head with no face and no hair, just a single eye on top, looking up. Carl was terrified, thinking the 'thing' might crawl, worm-like, towards him at any time but then heard his mother's voice shouting from above the ground, 'Yes, just look at him. That is the man eater!' (Jung, 1963). Carl woke terrified, wondering what his mother had meant. Was she referring to Jesus, the devourer of children, or the 'Jesuit'? He reflected on his 'big dream' often throughout his life, deepening his understanding of its symbolism and meaning as he experienced more of life and developed his theories accordingly. In later childhood, he realized that it was a phallus he had seen in his dream and, from then on, Jesus, the Jesuit and the phallus became indistinguishable in his mind.

Through this dream, Jung believed he had been 'initiated into the secrets of the earth,' and into, 'the realm of darkness.' He acknowledged, 'My intellectual life had its unconscious beginnings at that time' (1963). The dream had activated ideas in his mind that he later developed into his theories around the archetypes of God and religion, a God that encompasses the archetypal polarities of good and evil, light and shadow, and so can be simultaneously revered, loved and feared. It sparked ideas about sexuality and the relationship between feminine and masculine, including the struggle for balance between the two that has played out throughout history and within our own psyches, as the anima and animus, our male and female energies and perspectives (see Chapter 3). Above all, it began Jung's fascination with dreams (see Chapter 5) and his ideas of the unconscious mind as a dynamic motivating force within us (see Chapter 4).

Secret Childhood Games

In 1879, when Carl was four, the family moved to Klein-Hüningen, just outside Basel. Like the vicarage in Laufen, the home was not a happy one. Paul and Emilie had separate rooms with Carl sleeping in his father's room. He experienced frightening and mysterious things around his mother's room at night, such as expanding orbs and ghostly figures that produced several detached heads, which triggered anxiety dreams of tiny orbs that grew into monstrous, suffocating objects. When he was seven, Carl began suffering from pseudo-croup and choking fits which, along with his dreams, mirrored how the atmosphere in the house was becoming 'unbreathable' for him (Jung, 1963).

To compensate for his fears and isolation, Carl created a secret world playing out fantasies that would make lifelong impressions on his thinking. In one of these games, he would sit on a large stone in the garden and declare, 'I am sitting on top of this stone and it is underneath'. He would imagine the stone's reply, 'I am lying here on this slope, and he is sitting on top of me'. He would then ask himself, 'Am I the one who is sitting on the stone, or am I the stone on which he is sitting?' This left him, 'with a feeling of curious and fascinating darkness' (Jung, 1963). Later, this childhood ritual would shape his insights into the importance of projecting in psychology, the idea that we can see the contents of our own consciousness in others (see Chapter 3).

In another game, Carl carved a tiny mannequin that he kept in a pencil case hidden away in the vicarage attic. He would visit his mannequin, bringing it tiny scrolls of paper, on which he wrote messages in a secret language. This ceremonial act brought peace and security that helped him cope with his father's irritable moods, his mother's depression and his own loneliness. Years later,

Fig. 3 Carl Jung, as a boy.

Jung learned how indigenous cultures, such as Aborigines in Australia, would present inscribed papers, sticks and stones to totems. Struck by the striking similarities between his game and practices taking place in far off cultures he had never heard of, he concluded that this must be due to an unconscious intuition shared by all humankind, shaping his theory of the collective unconscious (see Chapter 4).

The possession of secrets had a powerful influence on Carl. He considered this to be, 'the essential factor in my boyhood' (Jung, 1963). He never told anyone about his ideas about Jesus, the Jesuit and the dream about the man-eating phallus. His stone and the figure were added to the mysterious, inner world Jung kept to himself. The mannequin was the first attempt he made in trying to give shape to the secrets in his mind. Later, Jung would understand that the discovery of his patients' secrets was critical to his therapeutic framework of analysis psychotherapy (see Chapter 5).

School Years

Despite being such a big thinker, Carl did not enjoy school. The other children misunderstood and alienated him, fuelling his solitude. When he was 12 and just about to finish his first year in secondary school, Carl was pushed to the ground by another boy so hard that he momentarily lost consciousness. When he recovered, he thought, 'Now you won't have to go to school anymore' (Jung, 1963). From then on, he would frequently faint on his way to school or when he sat down to do his homework. He stayed home for six months until he overheard his father telling a visitor that his son had epilepsy and would never be able to get a job and support himself. It was at this point that Carl realized he would face a lifetime of poverty unless he could achieve academic excellence, and he rushed into his father's study and began poring over his Latin grammar. He eventually overcame the urge to faint and returned to school. Jung later recalled that this episode, 'was when I learned what a neurosis is' (Jung, 1963). His fainting had been a subconscious means of avoiding the trauma he experienced at school and his neurosis became another of his secrets, one that he felt to be shameful, a defect. This insight, however, would go on to influence and inspire his psychoanalysis and therapy (see Chapter 5).

Jung's home and school experiences led him to develop an intensely introspective personality. He was forced to look inside himself for meaning, rather than finding it in the interaction with others. This led to his rising awareness that he had two personalities which he experienced as distinctly as if his body was occupied by two people. Personality 'No. 1' was Carl Jung as he presented himself to the world; the self-conscious schoolboy who couldn't do algebra. 'No. 2' was a wise old man from the 18th century. This 'Other' personality represented the inner Carl, the dreamer, ruminator and secret keeper with instinctive creativity and a deep connection with God. Carl also saw two personalities in his mother. Emilie's No. 1 was as a good mother should be: loving, warm, kind and hospitable with a great sense of humour. Her No. 2 was authoritarian, sombre and imposing and caused Carl many anxiety dreams.

As a psychiatrist, Jung came to understand that everyone has two personalities, he had just grown up more aware of them than most. 'In my life, No. 2 has been of prime importance, and I have always tried to make room for anything that wanted to come from within.' (Jung, 1963). Jung experienced a life-long struggle to resolve the 'play and counter play' between his two personalities. He later incorporated his experiences in his personality theory, renaming No.1 and No.2 the Ego and the Self and understanding that the interaction and reconciliation he had experienced between his Ego and Self formed the central dynamic of personality development (see Chapter 3).

Jung's relationship with his father deteriorated over his teenage years. The hypocrisy of the Reverend Jung's private disbelief in the religion he practised with such public respect led to growing pity from his son and frustration that his father was unable, or unwilling, to answer any of his questions about God. Carl believed that his No. 2 personality was given direct access to the mind of God through his dreams and visions, something that was denied to his father. He began to lose any sense of unity with the Church, something he called, 'the greatest defeat in my life, and realized that an abyss had opened between himself and his father that he 'saw no possibility of ever bridging' (Jung,1963). As a result, Carl had no desire to follow the traditional family path into theology, instead developing interests in the humanities and science. Reverend Jung died in 1896, during Carl's first year studying natural science and medicine at Basel University. Having seen how her husband and son's escalating misunderstandings had the danger of becoming a hindrance, Emilie admitted, 'he died in time for you' (Jung, 1963).

Basel University

Shortly after beginning his university studies, during his early twenties, Jung experienced a pivotal dream. He was walking in a strange place at night, surrounded by a dense fog and struggling to move forward against a strong wind. Cupped in his hands was a small light that he felt compelled to protect, no matter how frightened or endangered he felt. Suddenly, he was aware of a huge dark figure looming behind him. He became aware that this was a spectre, Brocken, his own shadow on the swirling mist, created by the light he was carrying. The light was his consciousness, small and fragile in comparison to the darkness, but his sole and greatest treasure. This dream was a turning point for Jung, enabling him to realize that No. 1 was the bearer of light and had to move forward now into the responsibilities of study, finding a career and coping with confusions, errors and defeats. The strong wind was the past, pushing against his progress. The shadow was No. 2, and it became clear to Jung that he had to leave this personality behind, although never to deny his existence or declare him invalid. This dream was a precursor for Jung's idea of the shadow self (see Chapter 3).

Following this dream and his father's death in 1896, Carl emerged from his social isolation and joined the Basel student branch of the Zofingia Society, a discussion club for the sharing of ideas. He soon discovered a talent to excite and influence people with the originality of his theories, and his presentations attracted large audiences and dynamic discussions. During this time, Carl had a growing interest in the occult and spiritualism which was, in part, fuelled by some strange experiences he shared with his mother when a table in their home split straight through solid wood and a bread knife snapped into several pieces. Jung was at a loss to explain either event but, shortly afterwards, heard of relatives who had been practising table-turning and seances with a medium and who believed tapping noises to be communications from the other side. Seeing connections between these things and the strange phenomena in the house, Carl began attending seances held by his young cousin, Hélène Preiswerk. He was struck by how real Hélène's spirits seemed to her. She would insist she could speak to them and touch them as naturally as she could any human. Carl was also fascinated by the way a different personality emerged from Hélène when she was in a trance. 'Ivenes' was a dignified lady who spoke in High German in place of Hélène's normal Basel dialect, and Carl concluded that the seances enabled a mature, adult personality to develop in Hélène's subconscious.

Carl attended Hélène's séance sessions over a period of two years, making close observations of her behaviour as she became entranced. He concluded that Ivenes represented Hélène's adult self, developing within her subconscious. The seances provided Hélène with a space to develop and express her maturity. Jung presented his findings as the basis of his doctoral dissertation, 'On the Psychology and Pathology of So-Called Occult Phenomena' (published in 1902). This dissertation held the origins of two central ideas in Jung's analytical psychology. The first is that 'complexes', or different aspects of our personality, can 'personate', taking on different human forms through dreams, trances and hallucinations, The second is that most of the process of personality development happens at an unconscious level (see Chapter 4).

Jung's time observing Hélène helped him to develop a fascination with the human mind, something he was struggling to find in other areas of his medical studies. Then, shortly before qualifying as a doctor, he came across Krafft-Ebing's *A Textbook of Insanity* (1879), which was the first extensive textbook for psychiatry, the medicine of the mind, and provided the first systems for categorizing and classifying mental disorders. Carl read about psychoses as 'diseases of the personality' and it excited him so much that his, 'heart began to pound and I had to stand up and draw a deep breath'. So powerful was his sudden excitement that he concluded, 'It had become clear to me, in a flash of illumination, that for me the only possible goal was psychiatry' (Jung, 1963). In psychiatry, Carl had, at last, found a discipline that excited him and one where he could marry his passions for biological and spiritual explanations of thought and behaviour.

Apprenticeship with Eugen Bleuler

At the end of 1900, at the age of 25, Carl took up a post at Burghölzli Mental Hospital in Zürich as assistant to the eminent psychiatrist, Eugen Bleuler (1857–1939), the man who, in 1908, invented the term 'schizophrenia' to explain a group of patients who shared similar patterns of psychosis. Throughout his apprenticeship, Jung was driven by the question, 'What actually takes place inside the mentally ill?' (1963). He felt his colleagues were too fixated on symptoms, statistics and 'rubber-stamped' diagnoses, failing to care for their patients' individual stories and experiences. Jung had a very different approach, quickly understanding that, 'if I know his secret story, I have a key to his treatment.' (1963)

With his novel approach to listening to what his patients said, and making careful observations of their behaviours, Jung was able to show that their delusions, hallucinations and gestures were not just madness to be written off and labelled, but were full of personal, psychological meaning. One example was an old lady who had spent 50 years in the hospital making repetitive movements that resembled sewing. Jung discovered that her illness had come about after being jilted by her lover, a cobbler. Jung began to develop methods, such as the use of 'word-association tasks', a means of accessing the patient's unconscious mind by giving them a word and asking them to say the next word that comes to their mind. This was based on the idea that our unconscious can, sometimes, control our will and reveal something about the memories, including the trauma, repressed there. Jung created a list of 100 words and short phrases, including 'child', 'false' and 'to choose', to uncover stories and enable his patients to understand things that had been buried deep in their unconscious. For many, this proved to be the step that would lead to their recovery. (See Chapter 2 for a more detailed discussion of Jung's work in word-association.)

Carl's Marriage to Emma Rausenbach

The inner mind of mental illness was not the only focus of Jung's attention during his apprenticeship. He was also enjoying a courtship with Emma Rausenbach (1882–1955), the daughter and heiress of one of Switzerland's wealthiest industrialists. Emma first caught Jung's eye from the top of a staircase at a Zürich hotel in 1896. Although she was just 15, Jung told a friend, 'That girl is my wife' (Black BBC Interview, 1955).

In 'Marriage as a Psychological Relationship' (1925), Jung argues that relationships with parents can have a direct impact on one's choice of spouse. He held that most typical marriages

Fig. 4 Emma Jung.

were a union between one party who enjoyed a positive relationship with their parents and the other party in the marriage, 'burdened with hereditary traits that are sometimes very difficult to reconcile.' (Jung, 1954). He believed the psychological drain of managing this burden caused great strain on a marriage. Jung's own marriage certainly aligned to this theory. Emma was close to her parents and her happiness was their priority. Although Jung was a penniless psychiatrist, the least respected of medical disciplines at the time, her wealthy family encouraged the love match.

Jung only gives two passing references to Emma in his memoir (Jung, 1963), however letters between them paint a romance filled with 'colour and beauty' (Brome, 2001). Emma refused Jung's first proposal, but the couple eventually married on Valentine's Day, 1903. The union brought about an end to Jung's financial troubles. Emma's fortune enabled a more luxurious lifestyle, centred around an elegant family home overlooking Lake Zürich, built to their design. The importance of the woman Jung referred to as his 'queen' and the 'foundation of my house' is often overlooked. She funded and collaborated on Jung's work, and eventually applied it to develop her own career as a psychoanalyst, something Jung was very keen to encourage. Emma was also described as an excellent mother and housekeeper; an 'exceptional woman'. She charmed his colleagues, including Bleuler who called her 'a very good choice' for his prodigy (Brome, 2001). Once an isolated child, Jung enjoyed the active social life that came as his career blossomed, revelling in the company of people who could provide stimulating conversation. He hated parties for the sake of parties, however, and would often get bored and skulk away, leaving Emma to host alone.

Emma became pregnant within their first year of marriage and their first child, Agatha (Gret), was born in December 1904, followed by Anna in 1906, Franz in 1908, Marianne in 1910 and Emma in 1914.

Jung's Friendship with Freud

The year 1905 brought about dramatic changes for Jung. Just as he was adapting to family life, he was promoted by Bleuler to lecturer in psychiatry at the University of Zürich and to senior physician in the Psychiatric Clinic. This gave Jung opportunities to work on his theories around psychosis and schizophrenia and develop his therapeutic approach. He soon gained a significant reputation as a research psychiatrist, publishing his theories in respected medical journals and at conferences and presentations. His experimental findings were consistent with work on repression in the unconscious mind as put forward by Sigmund Freud (1856–1939), the esteemed psychoanalyst.

Jung sent Freud a copy of his book, *Studies in Word-Association*, when it was published in 1904. Freud believed human behaviour is largely influenced by unconscious memories, ideas, thoughts and urges. Traumatic experiences are repressed deep in the unconscious mind, but these memories can be activated, without any conscious control, by trigger events in our environment, causing reactions such as aggression and hysteria. Freud also believed our 'libido', or sexual urge, was the driver of all human behaviour and repressed sexual desires was a key factor in psychiatric disorders. Freud was excited by Jung's work and invited him to visit in Vienna in March 1907. The two got on so well that they talked non-stop for 13 hours, starting a friendship that lasted for nearly six years.

Freud quickly recognized Jung's potential to make a significant contribution to psychoanalytic theory and practice, and came to see him as a potential successor as leader of the psychoanalytic movement. He made Jung the first president of the International

Psychoanalytic Association on its conception in 1910, and chief editor of the first psychoanalytic journal, *The Jahrbuch*.

In turn, Jung came to see Freud as the man his father, the doubting theologian, had failed to be. Freud was a distinguished, respected and intellectually courageous mentor. Jung saw him as the father-figure who could help him overcome the uncertainties he still held from his troubled adolescent years, and to embrace his own masculine authority. Equally, Freud needed a 'son' but one who would be willing to accept his complete authority and, without any variation, continue with his ideas and principles. However, two of Freud's ideas were becoming particularly impossible for Jung to accept. Freud insisted that human motivation is purely driven by sex. Jung agreed that behaviour is driven by energy, 'libido,' but believed this to be a more general life force, with sexuality as just one of many driving factors. To Freud, the unconscious mind was entirely unique to each individual, whereas Jung believed in a deeper level of 'collective unconscious' that was common to all. He saw this collective unconscious as holding the entire psychic heritage of humanity, including shared myths, symbols, images and archetypes, on which each individual could build their own individual life experiences (see Chapter 4).

Freud came to view Jung's unique ideas as resistance, and a rift opened up between them. In 1913, Jung resigned his presidency of the Association, his editorship and his lectureship at the University of Zürich. To Jung, the purpose of life was to find your own perceptions of truth and goals and follow a path towards realizing your ambitions, becoming a complete person in your own right; a process he called 'individuation'. Individuation was a painstaking life's work of exploring, understanding and reconciling all areas of one's psyche, everything in the unconscious mind as well as our conscious awareness. As such, achieving the process is rare and reserved only for those prepared to do the inner work involved. Most of us spend large proportions of our life 'unindividuated' with an unbalanced psyche, leading us into co-dependences, problematic familial and unromantic relationships, poor decision making and a feeling of aimlessness in life (we will look at this further in Chapter 5).

Realizing that his ideas and truths were not aligned with Freud, Jung knew that he could only find individuation if he was to work alone once more.

Jung's Muse

Jung's split with Freud led him into a spiral of 'inner uncertainty and [...] a state of disorientation' (1963). This caused tension in his marriage, but wasn't the only cause of stress and unease for Emma. Jung loved Emma throughout his life but, plagued by the early separation from his mother, he was unable to trust the love of one woman and needed others in his life to feel secure. The dual care between his responsible aunt and the maid while his mother was in hospital had resulted in a split in Jung's 'anima', the feminine part of his personality (see Chapter 3). He believed this split caused him to need two types of women throughout his life: a wife to create his home and raise his children, and a muse to share his fantasies and to inspire his work. Jung had many female admirers and followers, many of them current or former patients, whose attention he enjoyed throughout his career.

In the early days of psychoanalysis, with analysts paying close examination to their own dreams as well as those of their patients, it was common for professional boundaries to become blurred and confused. Antonia (Toni) Wolff came to Jung as a patient in 1910, after struggling to come to terms with her father's death. Jung, struck with her sharp intelligence and keen interest in mythology, gradually fell in love with her. Emma was told about Toni by one of her husband's jealous devotees. Jung admitted his infidelity and insisted his mistress and muse should be incorporated into his family, welcome in their home and at their table. Toni helped Jung define and name some of his best-known concepts, including anima (the feminine in a male), animus (the masculine in a female), and persona (the personality, or mask, we show to others). She also helped him prepare and write his many papers and books. Jung believed she was his anima, the female like-mind to his. Toni worked very closely with Jung as he developed his theory of psychological types, including his ideas about introversion – people who tend to focus their energy and mind inward into themselves, and extraversion – people who focus their energy and mind outwards and like to interact and be seen in the world (see Chapter 4).

Toni Wolff worked on her own 'structural forms of the feminine psyche' (published in 1958) based on Jung's typologies. She believed the feminine psyche is made up of four structural forms, or types; Mother (the caregiver), Amazon (concerned with objective achievements, goals, ambitions and contributing to society), Hetaira (the friend, companion, lover and wife) and the Medial (a woman's intuition, spirituality, healing, imagination and connection to the collective unconsciousness). Toni argued that, for women, self-growth and individuation relies on the understanding and integration of these four types. Her work encouraged women to understand their inner-most intentions and priorities, bringing together all four aspects of their psyche in striving for their goals. While, at the same time, arming them with the knowledge that not every society, time and culture would share the same opportunities for them to be realized (Molton & Skies, 2011).

In 1944, following a heart attack, Jung's feelings towards Toni Wolff changed. He no longer considered her to be his anima or his muse and withdrew from her emotionally. When she died in 1953, Jung did not attend her funeral, stating his poor physical health and overwhelming grief as his reason. Emma attended on behalf of them both. He told a colleague, just before his own death, that Toni had been the 'fragrance' of his life, while Emma was 'the foundation' (Lauren, 1975).

The Creative Illness

Although she reluctantly accepted Toni in their life, Emma was never happy with Jung's polygamy and, together with the split from Freud, difficulties in their marriage contributed to Jung experiencing a psychic illness in 1913, at the age of 38.

His illness began with terrifying visions of Europe flooded or frozen by Artic waves and himself shooting and killing the Teutonic hero, Siegfried: 'an incessant stream of fantasies had been released [...] I was living in a constant state of tension' (1963). Jung was having a breakdown, providing him with the golden opportunity for study and research. Once again, he turned inwards, giving No. 2 free reign to explore his unconscious mind. He utilized 'active imagination', one of the techniques he had developed in his analytic practise, and found two characters within himself, a beautiful young woman called Salamone, and Philemon, a winged old man. Jung came to view them as the embodiment of archetypes: the eternal feminine and the wise old man (see Chapter 4). Jung saw Salamone as his anima (see Chapter 3) and allowed her to inspire him to draw mandalas as a way of expressing his psychic experiences and transformation. Philemon became the embodiment of Jung's individuation, as the wise old man of Küsnacht. He meticulously wrote down every detail of what happened to him, publishing it first as 'The Black Book' and, later, as his famous *Red Book*, a leather-bound folio of observations with his mandalas.

Jung acknowledged this time as the most important in his life: 'in them, everything essential was decided […] it was the *prima materia* for a life's work' (1963). Indeed, Jung's observations and experiences during his illness further developed his theories of the Self, personality and archetypes, as well as his ground-breaking personality theory, *Psychological Types*, first published in 1921 (see Chapter 4).

Family Life

Jung emerged from his illness and his terrifying 'confrontation with the unconscious' when he was in his mid-forties. He returned to his routine of patients and work, along with his study of myth, philosophy and religion and writing papers on a new understanding of the unconscious. Jung's accounts of his childhood reflect characteristics of early schizophrenia, and some believe his creative illness could well have been a time of experiencing deeper symptoms of the psychosis, then healing himself through his self-analysis and therapy. His eldest daughter, Gret, recalled how her father would go through phases, sometimes playing with his children (though he was a sore loser and often cheated), other times not seeming interested in them at all. Jung often spent long hours in his study, appearing only for meals and demanding absolute silence while he was working. But, after his illness, 'everything changed, suddenly he was there' (1975). Jung enjoyed cooking for his family, especially breakfasts and would often take them sailing and on camping adventures on an island in the lake. He was never good at discipline and the children had a lot of freedom to do as they pleased. With five children, cousins and friends, it was a busy home, very much a contrast to his own lonely upbringing. Jung was said to have, 'a knack of getting on with people – when he chose,' and was once delighted when a postman stopped him to ask about his theories on psychology and alchemy (Brome, 2001).

Alchemy and Individuation

By 1920, Jung's work and reputation had attracted a large number of disciples and devotees, among them the *Jungfrauen*, women often described as 'vestal virgins' hovering around Jung, their sacred flame (Bishop, 1995). Beginning to feel overwhelmed by the attention, Jung set off on an expedition to explore different cultures across the world. His mission was to find confirmation of his ideas around archetypes and the collective unconscious. His journeys, taking him across India and East Africa, not only confirmed his mythological theories, but helped inspire his next body of work: the psychology of alchemy.

When Jung returned from Africa, he was gripped by an urge to create something solid and physical to represent the fantasies and ideas; to 'achieve a kind of representation in stone of [his] innermost thoughts' (1963). In 1922, he purchased land at Bollingen, beside Lake Zürich, and spent the next few years building a tower, a home that would fulfil his childhood fantasy of a 'castle keep' with a secret laboratory. His house embodied many ideas derived from his travels, such as a curtained-off space for withdrawal into meditation and yoga that he had seen in many Indian houses. Jung wanted a space in his tower where no one else would be allowed; an oasis, cut off from everything and everyone, where he could exist for himself alone and enjoy time being 'most deeply myself' (1963).

Here, he wrote papers, elaborating on his theories, and developed his work around alchemy. Jung was fascinated with the science of alchemy – the idea of turning base metals into gold – and set about applying its principles to the understanding of psychological projection, where elements of the unconscious are projected onto conscious interpretations and behaviours. Alchemy is central to Jung's ideas around the dynamics of personal development and transformation. He was one of the first psychologists to see growth as a lifelong process towards achieving life ambitions and becoming a complete person in body, mind and spirit. He called this the process of individuation (see Chapter 5).

Old Age

Jung continued his work on alchemy and individuation. He also developed his work in spirituality and mysticism, inspired by his travels to India in 1937. Through his late midlife and latter years, he travelled extensively; several times across Europe, to the UK, and also to America, to present his work at clinics and conferences. He became good friends with H.G. Wells (1866–1946) during visits to London. As Jung's following grew, many believed he could have taken the path of a spiritual guru had he chosen to. As the Second World War broke out in Europe, Jung was persuaded to stand for the Swiss Parliament by a group who believed his psychology could be useful in politics. He did stand as a candidate but was not elected. By 1942, his health was deteriorating and he began to cut back on his clinical practice and set to work assembling his papers into 18 volumes of 'Collected Works'.

Jung's 80th birthday, on 26 July 1955, included parties, a celebratory interview and tributes across the world. Four months later, Emma suddenly fell ill and died on 27 November. Their eldest daughter, Gret, recalled how Jung was quite lost without her. Later in the year, he invited Ruth Bailey, a family friend, to join him as a companion and housekeeper, asking her to, 'Come and see me out' (1960, letters). On 30 May 1961, after a peaceful and happy day, Jung sent Ruth down to the cellar saying, 'Let's have a really good red wine tonight'. These were to be his last words. Suffering a stroke and slipping into a coma, Jung died a week later, on 6 June 1961.

Carl Jung's Timeline

Carl Jung	World Events
1875 Carl Gustav Jung is born on 26 July in Kesswil, Switzerland	**1875** Civil Rights Act is passed in the USA
1884 Sister, Johanna Gertrud Jung is born	**1884** Mark Twain's *Adventures of Huckleberry Fin* is published
1886 Begins secondary school at the Basel Gymnasium	**1886** Robert Louis Stevenson's novella *Strange Case of Dr Jekyll and Mr Hyde* is published
1895 Enters University of Basel to study natural sciences and medicine; begins to participate in séances with his cousin Helene Preiswerk	**1895** Oscar Wilde is arrested in London for 'gross indecency'
1896 Death of his father, Paul	**1896** First modern Olympic games held in Athens
1900 Receives medical degree from University of Basel; begins psychiatric residency at Burghölzli Mental Hospital	**1900** British Labour Party is officially established
1903 Marries Emma Rauschenbach on 14 February	**1901** Queen Victoria dies aged 81
1903 -05 Experimental research on word association at the Burghölzli Clinic	
1904 Birth of first child, Agathe Regina	**1904** US engineers begin work on the Panama Canal
1905 Appointed assistant medical director at Burghölzli Clinic; begins research on schizophrenia; publishes *Psychology of Dementia Praecox*	**1905** Albert Einstein publishes his *Annus Mirabilis* papers
1905 -13 Lecturer in Psychiatry at the University of Zürich	
1906 Birth of second child, Anna Margaretha (Gret); begins correspondence with Sigmund Freud	**1906** San Francisco earthquake
1908 Birth of third child, Franz Karl Jung	**1908** Official launch of Henry Ford's Ford Model T
1910 Birth of fourth child, Marianne; becomes first president of the International Psychoanalytic Association; meets Toni Anna Wolff	**1910** First public radio broadcast takes place; George V becomes King
1912 Publishes *Psychology of the Unconscious*	**1912** RMS Titanic sinks on maiden voyage on 15 April
1913 Correspondence with Freud comes to an end; resigns academic position at the University of Zürich	
1913 -18 Period of 'Creative Illness'; work on Black Books begin	

1914 Resigns as president of the International Psychoanalytic Association; birth of fifth child, Emma	**1914** World War I begins
1916 First mandala painting	
1921 Publishes *Psychological Types*	**1918** World War I ends
1923 Death of mother, Emilie Jung	**1923** Walt Disney Company founded
1928 Begins study of alchemy	
	1929 Beginning of the Great Depression
1930 Finishes work on *The Red Book*	
1933 Becomes president of the General Medical Society for Psychotherapy	**1933** Hitler becomes Chancellor of Germany
1935 Death of sister Gertrude	
1939 Resigns from the International Medical Society for Psychotherapy	**1939** World War II begins; Freud dies aged 83
1944 Publishes *Psychology and Alchemy*	
1945 Receives honorary doctorate from the University of Geneva on 70th birthday	**1945** World War II ends
1948 Approves the establishment of the C.G. Jung Institute in Zürich	
1951 Publishes work on synchronicity	**1952** The Great Smog of London descends, killing over 10,000 people
1953 Death of Toni Wolff; publishes *The Collected Works of C.G. Jung*	
1955 Death of wife, Emma	**1955** US involvement in the Vietnam war begins
1957 Begins work on memoirs, *Memories, Dreams, Reflections* (published posthumously in 1962); publishes *The Undiscovered Self*	
1958 Publishes *A Modern Myth of Things Seen in the Skies*	**1958** The BBC television programme, *Blue Peter* is first broadcast
1960 Begins work on *Man and His Symbols*	**1960** The Beatles form in Liverpool
1961 Finishes last work 'Approaching the Unconscious'; dies on 6 June at home in Küsnacht, Switzerland	**1962** The Berlin Wall is constructed

2. Influences on Jung's Thinking

The depth and complexity of Jung's thinking, from his early childhood right up to his last days, was influenced by a myriad of cultural, religious, spiritual, philosophical, esoteric and clinical ideas. His unique personality and perspective gave him an astonishing, innate ability to take these ideas and ponder on them, turning them inwards and then applying them to his own thoughts and experiences. What he discovered from his own self-experimentation led to the development of his ground-breaking theories and therapies.

Nineteenth-century Switzerland

Jung was born in Switzerland at a time when 'women wore skirts which almost swept the ground, the family was sacred [...] religion [was in] all areas of life [...] and sex was regarded by some as an unfortunate prerequisite of reproduction' (Brome, 1978). Within such tight social constraints, instincts – such as aggression, self-interest and sexual desires – could not be easily expressed. Instead, they were repressed as unconscious thoughts and drives and became all the stronger and more powerful as a result. Freud believed this repressive climate contributed to the 'hysteria' he often saw among his female patients in Vienna,

Austria, at this time. Although he believed symptoms like fainting, paralysis and uncontrolled weeping to be caused by repressed traumatic memories, Freud held that suppressed sexual longings were also a contribution (1896).

Jung's own neurosis and hysteria, manifested in his pseudo-croup, fits and fainting attacks, can be seen as symptoms of the inhibiting atmosphere of disillusionment within his family. The Jung family dynamics would certainly have been at odds with the family life that 19th-century society idealized and expected, and was therefore something that the young Carl would have been unable to express or discuss with anyone. This led Jung to understand, from a young age, that there was more to life than could be consciously explained. It also contributed to Jung's dreams, where his undisclosed, unconscious mind was released, and to his understanding of the impact that the hidden secrets he had kept throughout his childhood could have had on his developing mind. Jung's dreams remained critical in driving his understanding and shaping his theories surrounding the unconscious mind, personality, myths, symbols and archetypes. Helping his patients to discover the secrets locked in their unconscious became the central component in his approach to analysis and psychotherapy (we will look at this further in Chapter 5).

Religious Beginnings

Jung grew up in a society dominated by religion of which there was no escaping, having a father who was the parish priest of their village. His encounter with 'the Jesuit' and his early 'big dream' gave him a great fear of Jesus and the Church but he remained

Fig. 5 The Jung family.

fascinated with God (see Chapter 1). This manifested through a rather amusing recurring daydream where Jung would walk past Basel Cathedral and look up at the building silhouetted against a sunny blue sky. He would imagine God sitting upon a golden throne in his heavens, high above the world. Then, an enormous turd would fall on the cathedral, smashing its roof and walls.

This vision gave Jung a sense that God was sharing a message with him. He believed that he had been gifted with the knowledge of the 'miracle of God's grace' (1963), understanding Him as an immediate, living entity, showing Himself to be free of His Church and less than perfect in His behaviour. Jung felt that God wanted him to 'sin' by thinking thoughts of God and his turd, encouraging him to break religious convention and take on new ideas about the relationship between humans and the divine. Jung knew that his father would never be able to understand this. Paul Jung could only believe in the God presented in the Bible in the tradition that his forefathers had passed on – beliefs that he no longer held himself. This led to Paul living a distressing double life, acting the role of parish priest in the absence of any personal conviction.

Throughout his youth, Jung had tried to discuss his ideas about God and religion with his father, not least in the hope that sharing the miracle of grace with him would help his father's depression and guilt around his loss of faith. But his father would always shut down the conversations, telling Jung, 'You always want to think. One ought not to think, but believe' (1963). This breakdown in communication drove Jung to pity his father and increase the rift that was growing between them.

Jung later revisited the idea of the imperfect God encouraging sin when developing his ideas of the 'shadow self' – the darker parts of personality that drive resentments and negative desires (see Chapter 3). Through his dream and the subsequent beliefs

that God wanted him to sin and feel the anger, disappointment and resentment that follows sin, God had shown Jung that He had a shadow too. Therefore, the religious conventions of ridding oneself of darkness and sinful thoughts to be 'pure' and 'Godlike' were unnecessary and, to Jung, counterproductive. He held that the more we try and push this shadow side of ourselves away, the stronger it

Fig. 6 Jung's Grandfather, Carl Gustav Jung.

becomes. Instead, Jung developed the concept and practice of 'shadow work,' a therapeutic approach enabling people to find and understand their unconscious shadow self and bring it to their conscious surface where unresolved issues could be worked on and healed. Jung came to see regular shadow work as a necessary, lifetime routine to enable the growth and transformation needed to reach individuation (see Chapter 5).

Goethe and 'Faust'

From his mid-teens, Jung found reading philosophy to be a welcome and valuable escape from the troubling atmosphere his arguing parents created at home. The ideas he discovered helped shape his formative thinking and later theories. His mother, Emilie, pointed the young Carl towards the philosopher and writer, Johann Wolfgang von Goethe (1749–1832).

Jung fell in love with Goethe's famous literary work, *Faust* (1808). The book tells the story of the devil, represented by Mephistopheles, who makes a bet with God that he can tempt Faust away from his good deeds. It explores various philosophical ideas surrounding man's struggle between good and evil, including the idea that goodness has an opposite side that is dark and malevolent. These ideas resonated with Jung's visions of God showing him his dark, shadow side and helped shape his thinking on religious archetypes and the shadow self.

Jung's grandfather, Carl Gustav Jung, was rumoured to be Goethe's illegitimate son. Though his grandmother, Sophie Ziegler, was a friend of the writer, there is no proof to this claim. The legend amused Jung. On one hand, he believed that his fascination with Faust may have been driven by an inner reality that the book connected him to his great-grandfather. On the other hand, he was annoyed by the story, calling it 'bad taste', reflecting a world where, 'too many fools tell such tales of the unknown father' (1963). There was no doubt that Carl Gustav held a strong physical resemblance to Goethe but the notion that the great poet and philosopher was his father is more likely to be legend than fact.

Plato, Kant and the Archetype

In his book, *Archetypes and the Collective Unconscious* (1959), Jung acknowledges that his ideas around archetypes are greatly influenced by Plato's 'theory of forms'. This theory holds that all objects are temporary and imperfect versions of their ideal forms which exist in a different realm – the Ideal Realm. According to Plato, this explains imperfections in our own world and why reality is constantly changing. Flaws drive change towards the ideal (Howard, 2000). Plato proposed that human principles, like truth and love, are ideal forms that we strive towards. We cannot see these things but our experience of them are central in defining our reality. Jung proposed that archetypes are similar to ideal forms in that they cannot be seen, only inferred from symbols and images, but are central to our perception and experience of reality.

Another philosopher who inspired and influenced Jung's ideas around archetypes was Immanuel Kant (1724–1824). One of Kant's most significant ideas was the suggestion of two types of knowledge. 'Phenomenal knowledge' incorporates the things we directly experience and come to understand through our conscious thinking and cognitive processing. 'Noumenal knowledge' refers to things that we 'just know' without being able to grasp how our knowledge of them came about. For example, we know to drink water when we are thirsty.

Jung's archetypes are similar in that they are essences of ideas that crop up throughout human experience; they profoundly influence our experiences without us being consciously aware of them. An example of an archetype is the idea of light and dark, as seen in the portrayal of the hero and villain in myths, legends and stories from all over the world, long before books and films were shared on a global level. This archetype still drives writers, set designers, composers and costume designers today, and enables their audiences to instantly understand, without conscious thought, the role a character will play in the plot, before it unfolds.

Archetypes provide a general formula that reflects the ancient ways of seeing reality that were initiated by Plato. Kant's idea of noumenal knowledge supported Jung's view that we come into the world with innate archetypes, giving us knowledge of things, before we even experience them. These have an important role in helping us navigate our world and allow us instinctive, evolved survival mechanisms. One such archetype is the law of causality, an unconscious ability for us to just know things like we will be hungry if we don't eat and will get injured if we touch fire. We will look at Jung's theory of the archetype in more detail in Chapter 4.

Arthur Schopenhauer

Jung discovered the work of Arthur Schopenhauer (1788–1860) through the time he spent reading books in his father's study.

Schopenhauer held a 'world view' that there were powerful forces at work beneath the surface of human life. Jung saw this idea in his own understanding of the unconscious processes that drive human behaviour. In his most famous book, *The World as Will and Idea* (1883), Schopenhauer proposes that each of us have an underlying, strong will, that can displace our conscious attempts to define our own path in life. Regardless of our own life goals, this fundamental will can come to the surface and pull us away from our individual plans in an instant. An example of such a will is the primary drive for us to procreate for the human race to survive and evolve.

Schopenhauer holds that we often have no conscious understanding of the origins of the deepest thoughts that drive our behaviours. These come from a deeper layer in our mind that we are not conscious of. This way of thinking was a powerful influence for both Jung and Freud. For Freud, the basic and unconscious will that drives human behaviour is sexual libido. For Jung, unconscious motivation was also shaped by creativity and spirituality.

Friedrich Nietzsche

The ideas proposed by Friedrich Nietzsche (1844–1900) had a profound impact on Jung. Nietzsche's philosophy centres around the idea that mankind is free of the influence of God, instead focusing on the individual wrestling with their own inner conflicts. Nietzsche coined the term *Ubermensch*, translated as 'Superhuman', to refer to someone who is able to take on the task of overcoming their inner challenges and weaknesses and push against the rationalist and materialist tendencies of the world. This idea was a direct blueprint for Jung's theory of individuation, the goal of man to grow and transform throughout life to become the best version of themselves possible and achieve balance between their life goals and their unconscious creative and spiritual motivations.

For Nietzsche, our task in life is not to accept knowledge without thought, but to seek our own experiences and interpretations of the world (Huskinson, 2004). This approach inspired Jung in both his clinical work and theories. Jung quickly grasped that helping his patients to access and understand their unique experiences, stories and secrets was the key to helping them, and their psychiatrists, to understand the cause of their disorder and point to a path of treatment and recovery. This individual view also drove Jung's understanding of his own psyche and personality and the development of his theories of personality and personality development.

Psychiatry and Word Association

Jung's work in psychiatry was strongly influenced by Eugen Bleuler's ground-breaking work on dementia praecox, the condition Bleuler would term 'schizophrenia'. Bleuler was the first person to distinguish 'psychosis' – delusional states and ideas the patient believes to be true – as distinct from 'neuroses'. The important difference between the two being that, with psychosis, patients lack any insight that their psychotic beliefs, hallucinations and experiences are not true in reality.

Bleuler believed that the patient could gain insight by achieving some separation between ideas that were 'me' and delusions that were 'not me'. Once these distinctions had been made, the patient could begin to release themselves from their psychotic ideas. As we saw in Chapter 1, during his apprenticeship with Bleuler at the Burghölzli Mental Hospital in Zürich, Jung's work there led him to begin experimenting with word-association tests to see if he could identify themes and patterns in patients' behaviour that would reveal what was going on in their unconscious mind.

In a word-association test, the clinician or experimenter reads the patient a series of words from Jung's standard list of 100 words and phrases (Jung, 1919). The clinician pauses after each to allow the patient to respond with the first word they think of. Jung was interested in the words his patients would give in response to certain, test words and how they paused before doing so. He believed that the longest silences indicated where the deepest conflicts and neuroses lay. For example, the word 'angry' could initiate the response of 'mother' of 'father' or may cause a patient that who felt guilt or shame to pause or fall silent. (Jung,

1. head	21. ink	41. money	61. house	81. deportment
2. green	22. angry	42. foolish	62. dear	82. narrow
3. water	23. needle	43. pamphlet	63. glass	83. brother
4. to sing	24. to swim	44. despise	64. to quarrel	84. to fear
5. dead	25. voyage	45. finger	65. fur	85. stork
6. long	26. blue	46. expensive	66. big	86. false
7. ship	27. lamp	47. bird	67. carrot	87. anxiety
8. to pay	28. to sin	48. to fall	68. to paint	88. to kiss
9. window	29. bread	49. book	69. part	89. bride
10. friendly	30. rich	50. unjust	70. old	90. pure
11. to cook	31. tree	51 frog	71. flower	91. door
12. to ask	32. to prick	52. to part	72. to beat	92. to choose
13. cold	33. pity	53. hunger	73. box	93. hay
14. stem	34. yellow	54. white	74. wild	94. contented
15. to dance	35. mountain	55. child	75. family	95. ridicule
16. village	36. to die	56. to take care	76. to wash	96. to sleep
17. lake	37. salt	57. lead pencil	77. cow	97. month
18. sick	38. new	58. sad	78. friend	98. nice
19. pride	39. custom	59. plum	79. luck	99. woman
20. to cook	40. to pray	60. to marry	80. lie	100. to abuse

Jung's standard list of 100 words and phrases used for word-association tests, taken from his
The Collected Works, Vol 1: Psychiatric Studies (1957).

1919). Jung noticed that such delays were often accompanied by physical reactions, such as exaggerated facial expressions and bodily responses to the instructions his patients were receiving. He concluded that these reactions were beyond the control of will. Instead, he proposed that they were indicative of complexes creating a strong, unconscious influence on the psyche and subsequent behaviour (Jung, 1957).

Previously, Jung had observed complexes, or part-personalities made up of separate unconscious components, through his work with Hélène Preiswerk (see Chapter 1). He proposed that complexes are constellations of powerful influences in the unconscious mind that motivate the individual's thoughts and behaviour. Complexes are made up of aspects of personality, early formative experiences and archetypes, all brought to mind by current events. In word-association, the words read by the therapist are the stimuli, or events, that bring complexes to the surface. When all the words that meet these delays and reactions are gathered together, it is often possible to see complexes through clusters of related ideas.

An example of this can be seen in Jung's work with a 65-year-old woman who was hearing voices and experiencing delusions of having inherited large amounts of money. The woman showed quick responses to many words, such as 3.4 seconds to associate 'butter' with 'bread'. Other associations were much longer. She associated the word 'thread' in response to 'needle', 'yes' in response to 'head' and 'Socrates' for 'pupil'. All these words took her between 11 and 15 seconds to think of. Through his testing, Jung was able to uncover a series of complexes associated with her perception of a difficult and hard life working as a dressmaker and frustrated dreams that clustered under her 'dreams of happiness', 'complaints of suffering injustices' and 'sexual complexes' (Ellenberger, 1970).

Freud

When the friendship between Jung and Freud came to an end in 1913 (see Chapter 1), a schism was created in the field of psychoanalysis and analytical psychology that is still felt today. Many current scholars and practitioners continue to believe that developments in psychology were forever hindered after the pair stopped working together. However, although the split led to Jung's illness, the surge of creation that came afterwards led to the Jungian model of psychology and therapy, something that may never have been possible if it weren't for his painful parting with his mentor.

Despite their deep disparities, there were aspects of Freud's work that influenced Jung in his thinking and theoretical developments, both before and after their time together. Having read Freud's *The Interpretation of Dreams* (1900) while working in Burgholzi before the pair met, Jung recognized his own growing ideas about complexes in the 'repressed wishes' and 'traumatic memories' that Freud believed could be seen in dreams and that were responsible for neurotic symptoms. It is at this point that Freud's work became vitally important to Jung and that these Freudian concepts began to inform his work.

Jung continued to build on Freud's seminal work on dream analysis, agreeing that dreams enable an invaluable window into the unconscious mind. Though he could not agree that everything in a dream must relate to unfulfilled sexual desires, Jung did believe

Fig. 7 Jung (front row right) and Freud (front row left) outside Clarke University, their American trip 1909. This was a turning point for their relationship, when discussions about dreams and unconscious revealed the differences that led to their split..

that they are filled with symbols that, when explored, can lead to understanding themes in unconscious thought and motivation. Jung developed his work on dreams to explore how the themes and symbols they contain can indicate where an individual needs to 'compensate'; where they need to change their attitudes and behaviours in order to achieve balance across the different parts of their psyche or personality. Jung also believed that dreams can contain collective symbols of archetypes, giving them a wider significance to the individual dreamer in contributing to the collective consciousness (see Chapter 4).

Jung also took ideas from Freud to develop his therapeutic practice. This included acknowledging the importance of the 'therapeutic hour' (50 minutes) as a strict boundary for psychoanalysis. Freud considered that sessions extending beyond an hour could become too long for a client to sit with their pain, causing trauma and an overwhelmed nervous system. It could also cause the therapist to become fatigued, unable to maintain a fresh perspective and at risk of becoming too immersed in their clients' lives. A period of 50 minutes allows time to wind down a session calmly, make notes and prepare for the next client. The therapeutic hour is a practice still held as vital to psychotherapists and counsellors today (Herbert, 2018).

Jung also adopted Freud's practice of 'free association', a practice where the therapist asks the patient to freely share any thoughts and words and anything else that comes to mind. Free association doesn't have to be coherent with obvious connections in the mind flow. Freud claimed free association gave patients complete freedom to examine their thoughts without any bias from prompting or intervention by their therapist. Jung used free association, alongside word-association, as a means of exploring the unconscious mind and eliciting recurrent and clustering themes to highlight complexes (Jung,1957).

Astrology

Jung spent a great deal of his time and his thinking in the liminal juncture between psychology, religion, spirituality, magic, mysticism and medicine. His theories and practice, though no doubt constrained by the dominant views of science and religion at the time, were influenced by all of these things, something that makes Jungian thinking so unique and intriguing. Jung sought psychological insights from esoteric ideas, especially astrology. Although astrology was considered to be occult in Jung's time, prior that that – up until the 18th century – it was such a mainstream discipline that it was a compulsory part of medical training.

Jung believed astrology could provide vital symbolic insights into the workings of the human psyche and that it had a significant importance in psychology, concluding that, 'astrology represents the sum of all the psychological knowledge of antiquity' (1930). Despite Jung's strong conviction, the influence astrology played in his theories and his application of astrological charts in his clinical practice are rarely mentioned outside specialist collections of his writings on the subject. Jung has an ambiguous reputation in the cognitive and biologically biased fields of psychiatry and clinical psychology. Historically, the absence of discussion of astrology as one of his most important influences may have been in fear that this could further undermine the scientific validity of his work. However, astrology has had a surge in popularity during the 21st century, with its ideas and symbols becoming common place in art, fashion and media. This makes it a good time to explore how Jung's thinking was influenced by his study of this ancient, scientific art.

For Jung, the astrological chart represents the symbolic portrayal of the archetypes, once personified by the gods and goddesses of mythology, at the specific moment of birth. He connects this with his theory of 'synchronicity' – meaningful coincidences where two or more seemingly unrelated events with similar meanings happen at the same point in time. For example, when somebody you have not seen or thought about for a long time comes to your mind, just as they phone. Jung believes that when a person experiences synchronicities, symbolic meanings and archetypes that are important in an individual's unconscious motivations are highlighted. The astrological birth chart was one such synchronicity and one that was rich in symbolic and archetypal meaning that could map an individual's personality and their path to individuation. Referring to his own personality trait of needing to understand the world and everything in it, Jung wrote, 'In my case, it must have been a passionate urge to understanding that brought about my birth. For that is the strongest element in my nature.' (1963)

In 1911, Jung wrote to Freud, 'My evenings are taken up very largely with astrology. I make horoscopic calculations in order to find a clue to the core of psychological truth.' Jung went on to outline to Freud how he had used a birth chart in one of his psychiatric cases. He found that his patient's chart contained many biographical details that described her mother. It is common in astrology to find repeated cycles and patterns among generations but the thing that interested Jung was that this patient had a severe 'mother complex' at the heart of her mental illness. Jung went on to use birth charts as a central part of his psychiatric practice, holding that they could enable, 'verifiable diagnoses' (1929). In a later letter to another colleague, Jung explained how he would often draw up a horoscope for patients he was finding difficult to diagnose. The astrological data enabled insights he would not have been able to gain and understand without them.

Astrological ideas can be seen at the heart of all of Jung's ideas and theories. He intuitively understood the 12 signs of the Zodiac to work as a compilation of psychic realities that configured the archetypes as psychological patterns that inhabit and inform the collective unconscious. Through the placing and relationships of these signs and the planets in a birth chart, Jung understood the symbolic portrayal of an individual's personality, purpose and destiny to represent and inform the understanding of Self, personality development and individuation.

Most of Jung's main theories, especially his work on archetypes and individuation and his idea of using birth charts in analysis and therapy, are still central influences for specialist counsellors and therapists today.

3. The Human Psyche and Personality

J ung perceived the human mind, or psyche, to be a complex layered system of consciousness and unconsciousness, as shown in Fig. 8. A central feature of Jung's model is the dynamic interaction between all of these different layers and how this impacts on our thoughts, attitudes, behaviours and our perceptions of ourselves and our place in the world. In this chapter, we will explore Jung's ideas about personality and how our sense of self develops throughout our lifetime. We will look deeper into his ideas of unconsciousness, the collective unconscious and archetypes in Chapter 4.

Jung believed that our primary goal in life is to understand and integrate all these different layers in our psyche. This enables us to expand our conscious experience, to grow as an individual and become the very best and most authentic version of ourselves possible. Jung called this process 'individuation', the process of becoming a complete person with a balance between our ego, our Self, our conscious, unconscious and our spiritual awareness. Jung equated this with the idea of transformation – recognizing and fulfilling our soul's destiny in this lifetime.

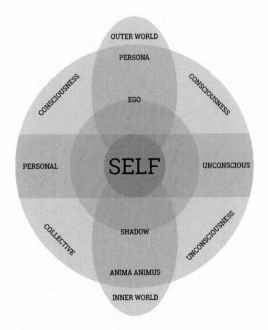

Fig. 8 Jung's Personality Functions

Self and Ego

As a young schoolboy, Jung came to realize he had two, very distinct personalities. 'No. 1' was Carl Jung's identity in the world – the self-conscious child who worried over his lack of skill in algebra. 'No. 2' was his inner self, the dreamer and ruminator. He saw similar distinctive personalities in his mother and later came to see the same in his patients. After his theoretical and personal split from Freud and his psychoanalytical movement, Jung was free to develop his own theory of the human psyche and personality based on these observations. Central to Freud's model of the psyche was the idea of the 'ego' – the centre of the conscious mind responsible for coordinating information from the outside world and unconscious processes that govern our response to what is happening around us. But this did not answer Jung's experience of two personalities and his struggle to rectify their co-existence. While he agreed with Freud that the ego was the heart of our conscious mind, Jung knew there had to be another aspect of personality at the centre of the human psyche, encompassing both consciousness and unconsciousness. Jung's 'No. 1' was his ego; his introspective 'No. 2' was his Self. The Self is one of the most important concepts in Jungian psychology. It is the central force in our psyche; the psychic nucleus that co-ordinates a lifetime of growth and transformation that enables our individuation.

The Self and ego are equally important to each other. The Self enables the ego to access unconsciousness, including the deep archetypal influences in the collective unconsciousness. It enables the ego to mature through the stages of life. A strong ego enables us to develop while maintaining our personal identity, feeling we are the same person at the age of 70 as we were at seven. To stay psychologically healthy, we need to keep the relationship between ego and Self in balance. When the ego over identifies with Self it can forget its place in the outer world and become over-inflated, thinking it knows best – what we call 'egotistical'. If the ego ignores the Self, it can become overconsumed with the world and become caught in all its trappings, perhaps making us become too materialistic or bury ourselves in work. The ego needs a strong sense of Self to give it depth, sensitivity and a sense of connection with our spiritual and ancestral past through the collective unconscious. A strong ego is equally important or it can become overwhelmed by our unconsciousness, leading to delusions and psychosis. This balance, termed the ego-self axis by Jung's followers, is an essential self-regularity process in the development and stability of personality throughout life.

The Ego

Our ego is who we identify as: the 'me, myself and I' component of our psyche. It emerges from the Self during our earliest stages of personality development in childhood. Jung used the words 'ego' and 'consciousness' intermittently, suggesting his concept of ego was the same as our conscious awareness, our perceptions of the world, and our place within it (Jung, 1958). Throughout life, the ego is dependent on the Self and our increased knowledge and understanding of our unconsciousness that leads to our individuation. Jung believed strongly that dreams are the portal to our unconsciousness and dream analysis one of the most effective ways to come to know and understand ourselves. When we are awake, our conscious ego component is the master of our thoughts. While we sleep, our unconscious is free to fill our mind with images, symbols and representations. Studying the content of our dreams enables us to understand the contents of our unconsciousness, gaining a deeper and fuller understanding of ourselves. We will explore the role of dreams in Jungian 'inner work' in Chapter 5.

Developing a strong ego is the first priority for healthy personality development. This needs to happen during childhood if we are to become an individual, to separate ourselves from our parents and to create our own life, career and family. Later in life, individuation requires us to be able to recognize the ego in subservience to Self.

The Self

Jung believed the Self to be both the architect and builder of the growth and evolution of our psyche through a lifelong dynamic interplay between our conscious experiences and our unconsciousness.

'The symbols of the process of individuation that appear in dreams are images of an archetypal nature which depict the centralizing process of the production of a new centre of personality [...] The Self is not only this centre, but also the whole circumference which embraces both conscious and unconscious; it is the centre of this totality, just as the ego is the centre of the conscious mind. (1953)

Thus, the Self is both the very centre of our psyche and also its boundary. This typically Jungian paradox can be difficult to understand but is best explained as the Self creating what makes us a unique, whole individual. The Self encompasses everything we are, while, at the same time, it gives us that sense of having something at our core, that something that we identify as 'our self'.

Another complex idea is that the Self creates itself in its own growth and development as it drives our evolution. It is who we have been, who we are and who we will become. The Self is the totality of our psyche and represents our understanding and wisdom of who we are. At the same time, it guides us in developing a deeper understanding: of bringing all the parts of our psyche together – conscious and unconscious – through the process of individuation, the realization of Self.

Jung was fascinated by repeating patterns, signs and symbols throughout nature. He observed that an instinctive feature of all living systems is to endlessly renew while maintaining the integrity of the structures that provide their identity. In the same way, the Self enables us to transform through life, while maintaining our personal identity.

Fig. 9 As a nautilus shell grows it maintains its structure, adding larger and larger chambers to accommodate growth. This is a great metaphor for Jung's idea of Self growth and development.

The spiral nautilus shell is a fantastic metaphor to illustrate Jung's idea of psychological growth and transformation. Life presents us with repeated challenges; we often recognize cyclic patterns in our evolution where unlearned lessons show up again and again until we finally learn what is needed for us to grow. Our line of transformation through life is not a linear one but a spiral; we cycle back and forth to revisit times of challenge and pain, each time with new insights from subsequent life experiences and our increasing awareness of our unconsciousness. As the nautilus grows, it maintains the same, repeating structure in its shell, adding newer and larger chambers each time. In the same way, we maintain our identity but grow and make space for bigger and fuller meaning and purpose in life.

The Amitayus Mandala

Jung saw the Self symbolized in the temenos or magic circle. The temenos is a Greek term meaning a sacred, protected space, within which alchemic transformations can take place. In a mandala, the temenos is contained and protected by the boundary of a drawn or imagined circular line. Just like the temenos, the Self provides a safe place where transformational mental work can take place. Jung developed this image as a squared circle, like a symmetrical rose garden with a fountain in the middle. Within this space, our conscious awareness can safely meet our unconscious, our Shadow, Anima or Animus, and all our representations and personifications of the archetypes in our collective unconscious. Jung likened

Fig. 10 Amitayus Mandala.

this to the image of the sacred mandala, an organised, geometric configuration of symbols representing the spiritual journey. He believed these could be used as illustrations of the human psyche. For him, the mandala is an archetypal image, found across culture and time that signifies the wholeness of the Self. Making a mandala enables us to represent and explore the conscious and unconsciousness parts of our psyche and to see it as a whole.

During his 'creative illness', following his split with Freud and difficulties in his marriage, Jung drew a mandala every day to explore and record what was going on inside himself at that moment. He wrote, 'with the help of these drawings I could observe my psychic transformation from day to day' (1963). Many of Jung's mandalas can be seen in *The Red Book*. We will explore more about Jung's use of the mandala with his patients and their benefits in self-discovery, individuation and therapy in Chapter 5.

The Self is our inner voice, it is what gives us the experience of a 'call' from deep inside us, telling us what we need to attend to, what we need to do, when we need to change course. It is intuitive and introspective. Our Self is the energy that drives us to achieve individuation, to bring our consciousness and unconsciousness together, to unfold and grow into the complete and authentic person we truly are. It is what makes us strive to be more aware of ourselves and others, more loving and wholesome. It is our moral compass. It is also our creative energy and our potential for what we can create in terms of our self-creation; everything we can create and bring to being in the world. As such, Jung believed there was an overlap between our image of Self and our understanding and perceptions of the Divine. We will see how this relates to our culture and religious archetypes in Chapter 4.

The Persona

In Latin, a persona is the word for a mask worn in ancient classical theatre to present a character to the audience. Put simply, our persona is the way we present ourselves to the world. When we encounter other people, it is their persona we see first. There is, of course, a little more to it than that, as Jung wrote,

> *'The persona is a complicated system of relations between individual consciousness and society, fittingly enough a kind of mask, designed on the one hand to make a definite impression on others, and, on the other hand to conceal the true nature of the individual.'* (1953)

Behind our persona, of course, is the rest of our psyche and all the conscious and unconscious information and processes coordinated by our Self. This includes our shadow – the part of our psyche we seek to conceal the most, that we least want anybody to see. The goal of the persona is to present a version of ourselves that is most acceptable and appropriate for each situation we find ourselves in. Our persona represents all the different social masks that we wear among the various groups and situations we find ourselves in every day throughout life. It is created through an interaction between our own innate and natural attributes and social, societal and cultural expectations and norms. For example, 'putting on a brave face' through adversity, having 'a stiff upper lip' and presenting ourselves according to our roles, such as how society would expect us to be as a 'perfect mother or father'. Our persona can be viewed as a mark of our success, or our willingness in adapting to others' expectations of us; from our parental upbringing, schooling and through messages on how we should behave received through media, marketing and social media. It enables us to navigate the different expectations placed upon us in our relationships, work and community.

A healthy persona is essential for us to be able to grow and adapt to cultural shifts through our lifetime and in the different situations we find ourselves, such as different friendship groups, societies and cultures. But by becoming too closely identified with our persona, especially with one of the masks it wears, we can lose sight of our true self. For example, becoming too dependent on the persona we wear in the workplace and struggling to cope with our leisure time, or losing our sense of identity after retirement, or over identifying as a parent and feeling lost in 'empty nest syndrome' when the children leave home to begin their adult lives. These situations can lead to psychological and physical illness, such as depression, anxiety and lowered immunity and can play a part in most diseases.

Over identifying with our persona can also cause us problems when two aspects of our world come together, such as at a party with a mix of work colleagues and friends we socialise with. If we have over identified with our persona, and not shown enough of our real, authentic Self, then which version of ourselves will we show in such situations – the responsible worker or fun and raucous life and soul of the social group?

Jung acknowledged that our persona is 'often rewarded in cash' (1959). Over identifying with it can cause us to become boastful about our material standing in life or feel the stress of 'keeping up with the Joneses', feeling pressure to have the right clothes, house and car to 'fit in' with those we feel are judging us. A weak persona can lead us to become too aloof and introverted, overly prone to retreat into our imagination and unconsciousness and vulnerable to delusions and psychosis. A successful persona needs to be flexible, enabling us to behave appropriately through our different circumstances through life, but still allowing others to see ourselves as unique and authentic individuals.

The Shadow

While our persona is how we most want to be seen, our shadow is the opposite. Through our persona, we do our best to present ourselves in the way we feel is culturally expected of us. Inside, however, we often feel that we have failed to live up to what is expected of us. This causes embarrassment, shame and pain that lives within our psyche as our shadow. Our shadow is made up of all our perceptions and experiences of hurt, shame, sin and guilt. It is everything that is weaker and less pleasant about ourselves, and everything we want to keep hidden from others.

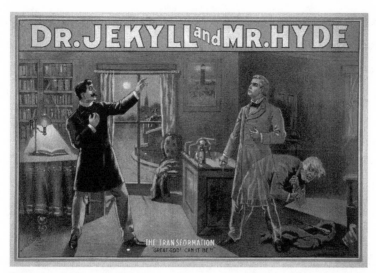

Fig. 11 Dr Jekyll and Mr Hyde can be seen as representations of the archetypes of persona and shadow in the human psyche or personality.

Our relationship between our unconscious shadow-self and conscious ego-self has often been explored in fairy tales and fiction. A good example is Oscar Wilde's *The Picture of Dorian Gray* (1891) with its handsome hero who has a secret, hidden picture depicting his malevolent secret life. Another example is Robert Louis Stevenson's 1886 novella *The Strange Case of Dr Jekyll and Mr Hyde*, about an upright doctor and his evil alter ego. The term 'Jekyll and Hyde' has become a household phrase for someone who seems to swing unpredictably between two personalities; someone who visibly shows their shadow.

Our shadow contains all the things that are unacceptable, not only to society, but also to our own personal morals and values. It encompasses everything about ourselves that we reject. It might include things such as envy, greed, prejudice, hate, and aggression. It also incorporates repressed and forgotten pain, trauma, ideas, negative desires, instincts and shortcomings; hidden dispositions that are present deep within the psyche of us all. We like to keep our shadow well away from our conscious mind, as looking at it and confronting it is hugely uncomfortable for us. We would much prefer it didn't exist. However, as Jung explained: 'The shadow is a living part of the personality...it cannot be argued out of existence or rationalised into harmlessness' (1959).

To become whole, to grow and reach individuation, we have to face our shadow, learn about what is there, bring it to the light of our consciousness and integrate it with the rest of our psyche. This is what Jung termed 'shadow work'; the 'act is the essential condition for any kind of self-knowledge' (1968). Without facing our shadows, accepting them and integrating them into our whole Self, we cannot become complete individuals and reach individuation. Our shadow will always create blocks, preventing us from reaching our fullest potential and, at times, may threaten to consume us.

Shadow Projection

Projection is the psychological mechanism of self-protection by placing the inner contents of our mind onto things outside of us. An effective way of seeing our own shadow is paying attention to characteristics that cause us instant and deep dislike in other people. We often deny these could possibly be elements of our own psyche and instead project them on others.

We may project our shadow onto people who openly express qualities that we find difficult to show. For example, if we take an instant dislike to people who radiate confidence, taking them to be self-centred and arrogant, it could be because something in our shadow has lowered our own self-confidence and caused us low self-esteem. We may also dislike people who display some of our own faults or our own unattractive or unhealthy ways of relating to themselves and others. For example, taking a dislike to somebody because they have a lot of money and we feel they are selfish with it, or don't deserve it, could be a projection of our own negative desires and shortcomings with money. Jung wrote: 'Everything that irritates us about others can lead us to an understanding of ourselves' (1963). Recognizing our shadow projection enables us to discover what in our unconscious is standing in opposition to our authentic Self and identity, and what is blocking us from reaching individuation and reaching our full potential. We need to recognize our shadows before we can begin the inner 'shadow work', which we will explore in Chapter 5.

The Anima and Animus

The anima is a female image and feminine aspects in the male psyche, and the animus is a male image and masculine aspects in the female psyche. These archetypal images are based on both the collective and personal unconscious. The collective unconscious contains cultural ideas about how men and women should behave, while our personal experience with friends and relations contribute to more personal ideas and images. For heterosexual individuals, the anima or animus can influence and inform the kind of partners they will be attracted to. The family maid who cared for Jung while his mother was sick mirrored his archetypal ideas of femininity. He was then attracted to these characteristics in other women with whom he formed friendships and partnerships.

In many cultures men and women are strongly encouraged to adopt traditional, often rigid gender roles. But Jung believed that discouraging and preventing men from exploring their feminine aspects and women from exploring their masculinity can undermine their psychological development. He viewed the anima/animus as representing important aspects of our true Self (rather than the persona, the image we present to others), serving as our primary source of communication with the collective unconscious.

The anima/animus exists in our deepest unconsciousness and can often be concealed by our shadow. It may only become accessible to our consciousness after we have done a lot of inner work towards our individuation and transformation and have begun to integrate our psyche. Synergizing our animus into the rest of our psyche represents the completion, unification and wholeness that comes when male and female merge together.

Jung believed a positive and healthy anima or animus was essential if we are to have a healthy relationship with the opposite sex. Like with our shadow, we can project our anima or animus onto others. Difficult early experiences with the opposite sex, such as a poor relationship with our mother or father, can cause us to develop unhealthy archetypal representations and complexes that we then project onto others, making us believe that they will cause us the same upset or harm.

Jung also talked of a healthy anima or animus bringing us balance in the gender characteristics of his time, for example a strong anima can help a man to be more sensitive and reflective, and a strong animus could help a woman to be more rational in her thinking. Although these ideas have become outdated, Jung's theory has provided an innovative framework for psychotherapy and gender study. It is important to see Jung's ideas of the anima and animus within the context of his time. Modern Jungian theorists and practitioners are now looking beyond this binary opposition of male and female with a view of revising his ideas to match contemporary understandings of gender.

Jung's Personality Types

In his personal life and clinical world, Jung observed different patterns in the way people behaved and interacted with each other and their environment. In Jung's time, there was a great debate in psychology as to whether we were born with a predestined personality, with an innate nature, or as an empty slate, a tabula rasa, on which our personality was formed through our early childhood experiences: our nurture. Jung believed that we are born with an innate personality predisposition to be dominant in either Extraversion or Introversion. This gives us a dominant 'general attitude type' that dictates whether we direct most of our energy and creativity outward, towards the external world (Extraversion, or E) or inward, towards our own inner minds (Introversion, or I).

Jung identified four global functions which he believed impact how we engage with life, Thinking (T), Feeling (F), Sensation (S), Intuition (often shown as iNtuition or N, to prevent confusion with Introversion). He categorized Thinking and Feeling as rational functions and Sensation and Intuition as irrational. Rational thinking and feeling are governed by the brain and based on logic and reason. Irrational sensation and intuition do not rely on logic and reason and is more heart- and emotion led.

None of us are completely introvert or extravert, rational or irrational. Jung instead visualized these as archetypal polarities on vertical and horizontal axes, as shown in Fig. 12. While some

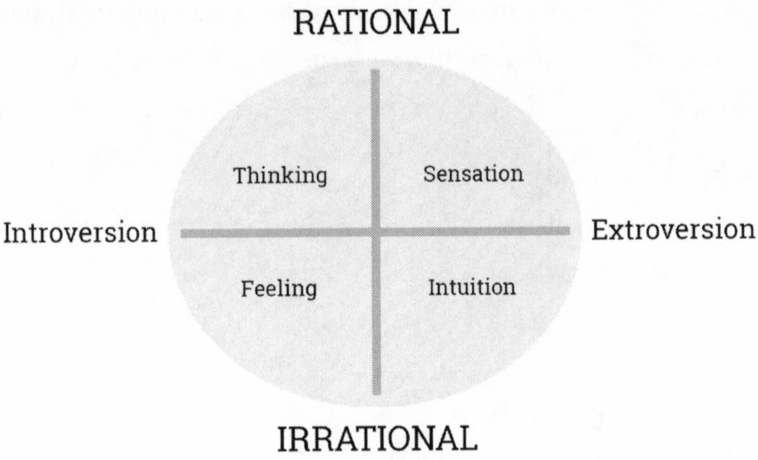

RATIONAL

Thinking   Sensation

Introversion ───────────── Extroversion

Feeling   Intuition

IRRATIONAL

Fig. 12 A diagrammatic representation of Jung's theory of the human psyche.

of us are extremely introvert or extravert, rational or irrational, most of us will be somewhere in between the two extremes.

Jung believed that while we use all the functions – thinking, feeling, intuition and sensation – we all have a dominant personality function that most defines our thoughts, attitudes and motivations. Our 'functional type' underpins our personality development and growth throughout life. Jung identified eight personality types:

1. Extraverted Thinking

2. Introverted Thinking

3. Extraverted Feeling

4. Introverted Feeling

5. Extraverted Sensation

6. Introverted Sensation

7. Extraverted Intuition

8. Introverted Intuition

According to Jung, we all have complex psychologies, meaning the different personality types will always be present to some degree and there can never be a pure type. He never intended his theory to be used to label people, more to guide us to understand what our dominant function is and what functions we may have buried that are underused deeper inside us. If we identify as an Extraverted Thinker (ET), for example, our less developed Introverted (I) or Feeling (F) side will still reside repressed in our unconscious. Jung believed that our repressed traits often appear to us in dreams. This can be useful in enabling us to see how we could make conscious use of these traits in our life and is another reason dream analysis can be so powerful in self-understanding and development. The process of individuation, of becoming aware and making use of our whole psyche demands us to understand these underused aspects of ourselves. We need to make use of all these aspects of personality to become a complete and rounded individual.

Extraverted and Introverted Thinking

Extraverted Thinkers are those with a preference for objective, rational thought results, based on fact and science. As extraverts, they direct their knowledge outwards into the world, looking for tangible results, perhaps becoming educators or working in engineering, science or business. In our society, this type is most widely validated because ETs utilize objective data and produce tangible results.

Introverted Thinkers are the great philosophers in life. They too prefer objective, rational thinking but turn this learning inward, ruminating, brooding, perhaps developing their own ideas. They may be lifelong learners but struggle to communicate and present their knowledge to others.

Extraverted and Introverted Feeling

Extraverted Feelers find it easy to express their feelings, making them affable and accommodating people. Their feelings tend to come from, and are directed at, what is outside of them rather than their inner mind. This can drive them to be swayed by public feeling rather than examining their own authenticity and values about things.

Introverted Feelers are characterized by the proverb, 'Still waters run deep'. They are driven by their own emotions and feelings and can find these difficult to communicate and share, making them sometimes quiet and difficult to get to know unless they can learn to translate their ideas and feelings into something others will also understand and feel. Otherwise, they can come across quite shy and aloof.

Extraverted and Introverted Sensation

Extraverted Sensing personality types value most what exists in the reality of their five main senses. They are not interested in personal subjective feelings or experiences. This makes them hugely practical, great at making and mending things and the kind of person who would love nothing more than inviting people to share a meal they have cooked. Their focus on physical gratification can make them susceptible to addictions.

Introverted Sensors are often life's artists. They can sense what is going on deep in their psyche and translate this into colour, texture, words, sounds and other physical form. While an ES artist would likely specialize in still life or landscape, IS artists are the great expression, perhaps surrealist artists, creating work influenced by their experiences of the unconscious. IS often bring everything they have experienced and everything they feel they could experience into their current moment and expression.

Extraverted and Introverted Intuition

Intuition refers to our capacity to get a 'sense' or a 'hunch' about something happening under the visible surface of a situation or about something that could unfold: 'a feeling in our bones'. Jung believed intuition to be a valuable function, especially for analytical therapists as it enables them to tune in to what is happening for their analysand.

Jung describes the Extraverted Intuitive type as having an 'attitude of expectation', always open for new experiences, opportunities and possibilities. They are often seen as inspirational people and can use their intuition to tune in with others, learn about them and direct and help them in their own lives. ENs make great aspirational, intuitive leaders but they have to be sure to live the life they prescribe to others, rather than jump quickly onto the next opportunity if they are to maintain their authenticity.

Those with an Introverted Intuitive personality type direct their intuition inward, towards their inner experiences. They are dreamers, impulsive people with great imaginations and so can be wonderful story tellers and creators of fictional worlds. Introverted Intuition supresses sensation which can make IE personalities struggle with reality at times. This can lead to uncertainty about how real a situation is in their life. Jung believed IE people who become too separated from their sense of reality could become susceptible to neuroses or psychoses.

Jung's Personality Types have underpinned all subsequent personality theories and the questionnaires and theories we use commonly today. This includes the hugely influential, Myers-Briggs Type Indicator® (MBTI) assessment, created by Isabel Myers and her mother, Katharine Cook Briggs. As we have seen, Jung's work is deeply introspective, esoteric, and spiritual. Isabel Myers started her own research and work on personality with the express aim of making a tool based on Jung's work that would be more understandable, practical and relevant for everyday life.

Myers took Jung's ideas of how our psychological types relate to our perception, attitudes and judgements about the world and created a series of self-report questions to measure attitudes and reactions. These show how Jung's types manifest together – which are dominant, which less so and what that means for the kind of personality we display, what our strengths are and what are those things that we find more challenging. The underlying assumption of the MBTI is that we all have preferences in the way we perceive and interpret our experiences, based on personality types, which underpin our motivations, values, needs and interests. The MBTI is a useful tool that is still used today as a measure for self-understanding and in practical settings. For example, it is often used in the workplace to help put together balanced teams representing different strengths and ways of thinking about things, enabling a wider, more holistic approach to a project.

4. The Personal and Collective Unconsciouses

The idea that our thinking and behaviour is fundamentally shaped and informed by experiences beyond our conscious awareness underpins all Jung's theory of the human psyche (see Chapter 3) along with his ideas on inner work and psychoanalytic practices, which we will look at further in Chapter 5. Jung was three years old when he began to realize his dreams were gateways to an unconscious realm of understanding that influenced his thoughts, attitudes and behaviours. He remained a great pioneer of the unconscious, dedicating his life to delving into the depths of his own mind and pushing himself to the brink of a psychological breakdown. By doing so, he was able to develop and test his groundbreaking theories, including his theory of individuation and his most important contribution of all – the concept of the collective unconscious and the archetypes contained there.

Unconsciousness and Individuation

Freud, and his followers in the psychoanalytic movement, believe the conscious mind to be like the tip of an iceberg poking into vision above the ocean. Underneath is a deep, wide chasm of experiences and memories that have been repressed through trauma or simply forgotten about. Freud believes that this hidden, unconscious mind triggers our reactions to the people around us and situations we find ourselves in. For example, childhood jealousy could lead to repressed feelings of inadequacy which would then drive outbursts of resentment or anxiety during adulthood. Freud believes we have no conscious motivation for these behaviours or any thoughts of where they came from. The influence of the unconscious on behaviour is automatic and outside of our control; our adult experiences and behaviours are predetermined by our experiences in childhood.

Jung's idea of the unconscious is far more than just a storage of memories leading to a set of reflexive responses. For him, the unconscious mind is a dynamic, active layer of the human psyche. The function of our conscious mind is to make sense of ourselves and the world around us and to work out how to think, respond and behave accordingly. For this, we draw on sensory information from the things we see, hear, smell, touch, taste and sense around us. To process all of this and understand its personal meaning for us, we also need to draw on our own experiences, the things we hold in our unconsciousness. Our conscious mind constructs our own, unique reality, based on the information it simultaneously receives from the outer world and the inner world of our unconsciousness. This can become overwhelming for our consciousness. When there is too much going on outside or within ourselves, things can easily slip from our awareness and we forget about them. When an experience overwhelms us emotionally, our psyche pushes it down from our awareness and it becomes a repressed memory. These are the things Jung believes form the shadow within our personal unconsciousness.

Jung strongly believes our most important task is to embark on a life-long journey of self-discovery and self-growth and development. Our mission is to find out who we are, what our purpose in life is, and to become as much that person as we possibly can in our lifetime. He calls this task individuation – 'the process by which a person becomes a psychological in-dividual... or whole' (Jung, 1959). Becoming this whole and complete individual necessitates understanding our unconscious processes as 'they must surely belong to the totality of the individual' (Jung, 1959). It is our lifelong responsibility to pay attention to our unconsciousness, to explore it, to notice how its contents impact on our conscious experiences and integrate these suppressed and forgotten experiences into our awareness. The key to being able to understand and follow our ambitions and reach our full potential in life lies in remaining attentive to what is going on within our unconsciousness, analyze its contents and learn lessons from the things suppressed there.

Jung acknowledges that individuation isn't always going to be easy. It is a process of 'many stages and is subject to many vicissitudes', variations and changes. Freud often illustrates his idea of the unconscious as an iceberg: frozen and static under the surface. For Jung, the unconscious is more like a stormy sea that can consume us at times, like when we become overwhelmed by the waves of our complexes. In order to reach individuation, we have to become mariners of our own unconscious mind. In Chapter 5, we will explore Jung's ideas on how we can best navigate this dark sea of our unconsciousness through our dreams, our imagination, and through psychoanalysis and therapy.

The Collective Unconscious

Jung's idea of the unconscious as a dynamic and accessible part of the human psyche is an important factor in his theoretical, and later personal, break with Freud. A bigger departure came with Jung's ground-breaking thesis that unconsciousness as unique and individual is simply 'a more or less superficial layer' (1959). Jung calls this layer the 'personal unconscious'. Under it is a deeper layer 'which does not derive from personal experience and is not a personal acquisition but is inborn' – the 'collective unconscious' (1959). The idea of the collective unconscious is Jung's most original and controversial contribution to personality theory and is viewed by most as his most significant contribution to psychology. This 'collective' part of the unconscious is universal to all mankind, across all time and place, containing identical information for us all.

> '*The collective unconscious comprises in itself the psychic*
> *life of our ancestors, right back to the earliest beginnings.*
> *It is the atrix of all conscious psychic occurrences.*' (1953)

Jung first became aware of this universal shared intuition when he realized the striking similarities between his childhood game of writing messages for his secret mannequin in the attic, and ceremonial scrolls presented to totems in Aboriginal Australia (see Chapter 1). This was a time long before the young boy could have seen images on television and in the media to influence his play. Later, Jung saw themes and characters repeating themselves in dreams, imaginations and hallucinations of patients from different backgrounds, again with no access to any media that could have given them shared scenes to draw from. Like many of his ideas, it was dreams that enabled Jung to conceptualize these observations into his theory of the collective conscious.

The Dream of the Multi-storied House

Jung's 'multi-storied house' dream came in 1909 while he was together with Freud on a trip to the United States. In it, he dreamt he was living in an ornate and well-furnished old house but realized that he had only ever experienced the first and top floor of his home. So, he went exploring and found a darker and older part of the house, with medieval furnishings and a floor made of stone slabs. Behind one of the slabs was a hidden staircase leading down to a deep cave cut out of the rock. The cave floor was littered with the remains of a primitive settlement with broken pottery, old bones and two ancient, partly disintegrated human skulls. When Jung relayed his dream to Freud, his friend was only interested in the skulls and asked if Jung was carrying a secret death wish for anyone. But Jung believed his dream was an illustration of the human psyche. The upper floor represents the conscious personality, our personal experiences, the things we are aware of about ourselves and our experiences in the world around us. The ground floor represents our personal unconscious, the unconscious mind that is unique to us, the home to our repressed memories and personal shadows.

The hidden cave underneath the house, Jung believed to represent the 'world of the primitive man within myself' (Jung, 1963), the collective unconscious containing the shared experiences of all mankind across the globe, shaped over time from our earliest days.

The Power of Archetypes

The collective unconscious contains innate characteristics 'imprinted' into our mind through evolution. We are all born with biological reflexes and instincts that drive us to eat what tastes good and spit out anything too bitter, or to move our hand away from something hot. Ever since our primitive days, humans have naturally done all these same things, without being taught or shown how. They are automatic reactions we find ourselves doing without any conscious thought. Just as reflexes influence our biological response to the world, Jung proposes that there are similar forms driving our intuition and psychological responses. These include inherited predispositions such as our fear of heights, of darkness, snakes or spiders. However, more important than these isolated, protective tendencies are more complex aspects of the collective unconscious: a set of common mental patterns we all draw on to help us make sense of ourselves and the world. We are all born with an innate stock of memory traces that we share with every other member of the human species, from the beginning of our evolution right through to the present day.

Jung called these shared, ancestral memories and images 'archetypes'. Archetypes are powerful psychological structures and forces within the collective unconscious. They are essences or kernels of ideas, thoughts, feelings, roles, images and symbols that strongly influence our way of thinking, our attitudes towards ourselves and our way of perceiving, interacting and behaving within our world.

Archetypes themselves – these kernels and essences of thought – can only exist in the collective unconscious. Once they enter our conscious mind, they are given form and become archetypal images. Archetypes have carried the same fundamental meaning throughout mankind's history, across all the countries and cultures of the world. Archetypal images are influenced by cultural understandings and interpretations, passed down through generations and shaped by our own experiences. We see them represented by universal themes expressed through literature, art, and in dreams.

Let's take the archetype of the 'Hero' as an example. We all know that the Hero, or Heroine, is someone strong and courageous; someone who goes into battle with a real or metaphorical monster or villain (another archetype, of course) and wins, often learning life lessons along the way. The Hero(ine) is an important archetype; our own fundamental and instinctive drive to assert ourselves into the world and overcome the challenges we face there.

The first archetypal images and representations can be found in mythologies. According to Jung, the very purpose of these stories was to enable our ancient ancestors to communicate and share the experience of the inner world of the collective unconscious. In earliest Greek mythology, the Hero and Heroine archetypes were represented by any character who was half god and half human. The Hero(ine) archetype later evolved into characters who started at a position of weakness and overcame adversity through great courage and self-sacrifice. Hercules was famous for his strength, his sense of adventure and for becoming a great champion and provider for the weak. Hera, wife of Zeus – goddess of all women – became protector for married women.

We colour these archetypal images with our own experiences. For example, a football fan may see the Hero in an underdog player who is substituted into a match with little expectation and then scores a winning goal. A mother may see a Heroine in her child who is battling a severe illness but who is determined to put her pain and weakness to one side, go to school and complete her exams. During the Covid pandemic in early 2020, we all came to see Heroes and Heroines in all the medical staff and front-line workers that we saw in news reports, sacrificing their own health and safety to save those most sick with the virus. These are all examples of how our cultural and personal experiences give form to the archetypes in our collective unconscious as archetypal images.

Archetypes are seen in recurrent motifs and themes in myths, fairy tales and folk tales all over the world. They are what enable us to identify so well with characters and situations in our favourite films and novels.

The Purpose of Archetypes

Archetypes play an important part in influencing the attitudes and behaviours that we need in order to successfully navigate our journey through life to ensure our survival. For example, when we face our own adversities and challenges, Jung would argue that the Hero archetype within us is activated and we react instinctively with bravery.

Archetypes can trigger the emotional responses that drive our transformation and individuation. One of Jung's main four archetypes (discussed later in this chapter), 'the trickster', leads us to inner confusion which we are driven to resolve, learning important lessons about ourselves and others and enabling us to move forward and avoid similar situations.

Archetypes provide meaning, they tap into our inner world of emotions, help us make sense of them. They give life meaning, helping us to understand our thoughts and our motivations. They influence our passions, our fascinations with ideas, the kinds of people we want to be with and what we feel about them.

Jung outlined four archetypes (1953), the main innate archetypes of the collective unconscious. These are the archetypes of 'Mother', 'Spirit', 'Trickster' and 'Rebirth'. Each of these archetypes carry strengths, shadows and complexes.

The Mother Archetype

The Mother archetype is essential for our survival as it enables us to recognize our own mother as care giver and to know instinctively that she will provide for us and nurture us. Our early personal experience provides us with a conscious archetypal image of the 'mother'. As we grow up and become an individual, our initial archetypal image separates from our early experiences of mothering to include anyone playing a nurturing and caring role for others, 'mothering them'. We then develop our understanding of this archetype, both seeking The Mother and becoming The Mother throughout our lives. We may also adopt archetypal images such as the virgin Mother of God, Mother Earth or Gaia, Goddess and other mythical and cultural images of motherhood.

The Mother archetype is associated with caring, nurturing, sympathy and empathy, the magic authority of the female, wisdom and spiritual exaltation, growth and fertility and any helpful instinct or impulse that drives us to cherish and sustain ourselves, our creativity and the people and things we care about.

The shadow Mother archetype incorporates anything secret, hidden and dark, the abyss, the world of the dead, anything that devours, seduces, and poisons and all that is terrifying and inescapable, including fate.

Each of us carry shadows from our childhood, born out of moments when we felt the hurt of disappointment, rejection and other common upsets. Most of us can recall a moment when our mother figure caused us hurt, for example, when our mother, or mother figure, gave us a harsh, perhaps unfair criticism or reacted in a way to us that made us feel insecure or disappointed in them or in ourselves. The 'mother wound' is a common shadow that most of us feel to some degree. But for some people, their experiences of 'Mother' in their lives is overwhelmingly a negative one, resulting in a darker archetypal image. In some cases, this can cause a 'mother complex' – negative associations with female or nurturing figures which, like all complexes, can be projected onto others throughout life, leading to difficulties in relationships. There are examples of the Mother shadow in the 'evil mother' or 'wicked stepmother' throughout mythology and fairy tales. In Judeo-Christian mythology, Lilith is believed to have been the first wife of Adam – the original woman, before Eve. She was a demoness, a temptress who personified the darkness and unbridled freedom associated with the shadow of the Mother and the Anima archetypes. The Goddess Kali is a good example of an 'ambivalent Mother', combining light and shadow, passion, goodness and darkness, loving on one hand and terrifying on the other. The shadow Mother is a popular villain of fairy tales, such as in Rapunzel, Cinderella and Hansel and Gretel.

The Spirit Archetype

The Spirit archetype is our unconscious essence we colloquially call the 'human spirit'. Jung wrote,

> *'The archetype of Spirit, in the shape of a man, hobgoblin or animal, always appears in a situation where insight, understanding, good advice, determination, planning etc., are needed but cannot be ministered on one's own resources.'* (1959)

He believed that the Spirit archetype often appears in dreams, enabling us to benefit from ancestral wisdom within our collective unconscious. The Spirit archetype is also personified in the magician, sage, wizard, crone, mentor, doctor, priest, teacher, professor, grandfather, or any other person possessing authority. It is seen throughout mythology, fairy tales, literature, art and film. Merlin, the famous wizard of Arthurian legend, is an example of a mythical archetypal image of Spirit. Famous modern examples include Gandalf in Tolkien's Lord of the Rings trilogy, and Dumbledore in J.K. Rowling's Harry Potter books and films. Perhaps the best example of an archetypal Spirit is Yoda, the Jedi Master and mentor who first appeared in the film, *The Empire Strikes Back* (1980).

Fig. 13 Yoda, the Jedi Master and mentor, is an archetypal representation of the Spirit archetype

The mentor is one of the oldest images of the Spirit archetype, originating in Greek mythology. Mentor was the son of Heracles and Asopis. When Mentor was an old man, his friend Odysseus placed him in charge of his son, Telemachus. Odysseus was leaving for the Trojan War and needed the wise old man to watch over, offer sound advice, and be a father figure to Telemachus in his absence. Athena disguises herself as Mentor to offer her own divine counsel to the boy. In 'The Odyssey', Athena, appearing as Mentor, convinces Telemachus to stand up to his mother's suitors and go abroad in search of his father. Thus, we use the word 'mentor' today to designate someone who offers wise counsel in trying times, the central characteristic of the Spirit.

We often experience archetypes in dreams. The Spirit can be one of the most frequent as our own, unconscious spirit works out what we should do about situations and appears in our dreams in the guise of a mentor. The Spirit can appear as voices and feelings, as a ghost of a loved one or as an ancestor. It can also appear as gnomes, fairy like figures and talking animals and birds.

In shadow, the Spirit can be ambiguous and playful, switching between helpful and unhelpful in order to trick and test the hero or heroine. It can even be malevolent at times. The shadow Spirit can leave us confused about our inner wisdom or conflicting advice from others.

The Trickster

If the Spirit can be confusing, it has nothing on the Trickster. Even describing this archetype can be challenging because its essence is the very embodiment of contradictions. Jung describes the Trickster as, *'a curious combination of typical trickster motifs [...] his fondness for sly jokes and malicious pranks, his powers as a shape shifter, his dual nature, half animal, half divine, his exposure to all kinds of tortures and – last but not least – his approximation to the figure of a saviour.'* (1953)

This Trickster represents all the confusion, dualities and polarities that get in the way of our desire for clarity, certainty and stability throughout life. The Trickster is an unpredictable shapeshifter. It is a transitional archetype that we encounter whenever we are faced with boundaries, endings and crossroads that challenge us to grow through discomfort.

In myths and stories, the Trickster is the character who stirs things up and brings chaos to the plot. Its actions often cause an abrupt shifting in the story direction, frequently because of the distress it has caused. The Trickster does just the same in our lives, unsettling us, causing us discomfort so that we are forced to make changes, grow and transform. Our inner Trickster introduces the element of doubt into things we were once certain about, pokes holes in rigid boundaries and complicates situations by presenting us with an opposite point of view. It is the archetype that pushes us to question norms and move out of our comfort zone and known limits. The Trickster is involved in any situation where we find ourselves examining our ideas and assumptions or feeling the need to stretch ourselves into previously unexplored life directions. It stirs our existing thought and belief structures and sends us forward into new ideas and ventures.

Fig. 14 Our ancient ancestors created mythological stories based on archetypal images. In Greek Mythology, Hermes represents the Trickster archetype.

The Trickster has many forms, both human and animal. Its physical form varies in different religions and cultures, but it is always a comedy of opposites. For every good aspect of the Trickster there is an opposite shadow aspect.

In Native American stories, the Trickster alternates between taking the form of a coyote and that of a man. He tries to fly and become a god, with hilarious and disastrous consequences. No matter how hard he tries he cannot escape the human condition, showing us we cannot aspire to be something beyond our own human persona and form.

Hermes, the god of travel and communication, is the Trickster of Greek mythology. Born of both god and mortal, Hermes created a bridge of communication between the heavens, the Earth and the underworld and was the link between these realms. He was a thief at the gates of the worlds, a watcher in the night and bringer of dreams.

The chaos and disruption the Trickster causes tends to cast this archetype in a negative light. One of the central elements of this archetype is dualism. The Trickster is neither strictly positive nor shadow − it is both. The Trickster is known to embody divine qualities, while at the same time engaging in diabolical acts. It is an amoral character who isn't bound to standards and rules.

The Archetype of Rebirth and Transformation

Where the Mother, the Spirit and the Trickster are aspects of our psyche that we can personify in others, the Rebirth archetype is a process that we can't see or observe as it is entirely beyond the ability of our senses to perceive directly. According to Jung, 'One speaks of rebirth; one professes rebirth; one is filled with rebirth. […] We have to be content with its psychic reality' (1953).

Jung distinguishes between four different forms of rebirth:

> **Metempsychosis** is the transmigration of the soul. With this, life is prolonged in time by passing through a series of different bodily reincarnations. Jung related this to Buddhist ideas of an extended spiritual life sequence, interrupted by different physical reincarnations. Though there is no certainty that the psyche or personality will continue, there is continuity in karma, the accumulation of lessons learned, or not learned, through each lifetime.

> **Reincarnation** is rebirth into a new life in a new human body. Personality is regarded as continuous in each lifetime and can be accessible as memories, often experienced through a feeling of 'knowing', of 'déjà vu' – a feeling of experiencing something before, or a strong reaction to a new experience.

> **Resurrection** is re-establishment of life and human existence after death. The most famous example of this archetype is the resurrection of Jesus in the Christian tradition and the idea that our current selves will be given a new life in another realm after our death.

Psychological rebirth is the constant process of change and renewal within the span of an individual lifetime. This archetype was the focus of Jung's work on the development of personality and 'individuation', the process of healing, strengthening and improvement throughout our lifetime. We will explore this more in the next chapter.

Jung believed the four main archetypes come together and interact to give rise to 12 archetypal images:

Hero – the urge for adventure and to prove oneself through courageous acts.

Ruler – the urge for control and to create a prosperous and stable community or family.

Creator/artist – the urge to create things that will have enduring value, creating culture.

Sage – the urge for truth and justice, to understand the world and not be duped.

Innocent – the urge to be free to be oneself and to be happy.

Explorer – the urge for freedom to explore the world and experience new things.

Rebel – the urge for revolution, to overturn what isn't working and exert change.

Magician – the urge to make things happen and understand the laws underpinning the universe.

Jester – the urge to have fun, a good time and to live in the moment with full joy.

Everyman – the urge to connect and be equal with everyone.

Lover – the urge for relationships with others, with surroundings, with work, to be wanted.

Caregiver – the urge to love, protect and care for others.

All humans throughout time and geography share these images in our collective unconscious. We recognize them in our own personality and experience, in others around us, and in myths and stories across the world.

Archetypes, Complexes and Personality

Our affiliation with certain archetypes plays a large part in creating the unconscious view of the world that defines our character and personality. For example, some of us identify strongly with the 'mother' archetype, making us instinctive caregivers and nurturers – the kind of person everyone wants to be around when they have had a bad day. Others may not identify with this archetype very strongly at all and much prefer to travel and have adventures alone, than be weighed down with family and children to provide for.

Jung's word association work shows how complexes develop in our personal unconscious. They are groups of thoughts, ideas and impulses that share a common emotional tone, such as joy, anxiety or sadness. Jung's work in psychiatry shows how large and extreme complexes can have a damaging impact on our mental health, influencing conditions such as depression and psychosis. We all have complexes and, though unconscious, they exert a strong influence on our attitude to ourselves and our life and on our motivations and behaviour.

We form our complexes around our archetypal images. Every archetype carries positive characteristics and a, less desirable, shadow side. These influence the ideas, thoughts and feelings we have about that archetype and the complexes we build around them. For example, the 'hero complex' can lead someone to seek heroism or recognition and, in its strongest form, can lead them to create a harmful situation for others so they can be the 'hero' and save them. A 'superiority complex' is a more common defence mechanism that can evolve to help a person cope with feelings of inferiority. Over time, they can develop attitudes and behaviours that seem dismissive and disdainful towards others to compensate for their own overbearing emotions.

5. Inner Work, Dreams and Therapy

As we saw in the previous chapter, Jung was one of the greatest explorers of the human psyche whose journey into his own mind and observations of others led to some of psychology's most significant discoveries and theories. Jungian psychology is far more than a collection of ground-breaking theories. Jungian psychology is something we do, it is a way of making discoveries about ourselves, enabling the growth of our personality and psyche throughout life and, ultimately, of reaching individuation – the fulfilment of who we were born to be through unifying our conscious and unconscious and becoming complete.

Inner Work and the Quest for Individuation

Individuation means becoming more of who we are meant to be through learning to accept, use and grow from our whole psyche, including our complexes and shadow. This involves an active process of self-discovery and inner healing – the inner work that Jung believed to be our greatest and most important task throughout life. Individuation enables us to live the life we were born for, have our best experiences, understand the world around us better, and relate better to others. It is important, not only for us, but for others in our life and for the world. Jung believed that 'ultimately everything depends on the quality of the individual' (1957), meaning that if we all do the work to reach individuation – if we all become whole, unified individuals and the people we were born to be – then, collectively, the world will function better; people will understand each other and get along better, and the human race will progress the way it should do. Jung's idea of the collective conscious refers to a growing, developing collection of archetypes. Thus, individuation is important for our future in providing healthy archetypes and cultural representations to pass through the generations.

Jungian psychology can be viewed as a quest to find out who we really are, understanding our current Ego, our conscious self, and exploring the potential of our unconscious. To have our best experience of life, we then need to assess the difference between our current and potential life. We need to heal the wounds and explore the blocks preventing us from being the person we could be and bring all the parts of our psyche together – our ego, shadow and persona – to realize our potential. Jung acknowledges that this will not be easy or always comfortable for us. Not everyone will have the motivation or discipline to reach individuation. It demands us to be open and honest about ourselves, our experience and our role in everything positive and negative in our life. But, for Jung, this is the only way to become fully responsible for who we are in this life and to get the fullest and best experiences from the limited time we spend here. Jung strongly believes we all possess the tools for individuation and can take our own journey of self-discovery and healing.

Jungian Analysis

Jungian analysis is the psychotherapeutic approach based on Jungian psychology. Its central aim is to help the individual in integrating their conscious and unconscious. Jungian analysis can be useful in clinical and mental-health settings, as well as in general. It can help anyone in their journey on personal discovery, spirituality and in achieving individuation and living their best and fullest life possible, in alignment with their purpose. To even be considered for training as a Jungian analyst you must have completed 100 hours of analysis yourself. The training process involves another 350 hours of personal inner work, a painstaking, systematic process of bringing unconsciousness into the conscious mind so archetypes can be enriched with personal meaning and all parts of the psyche bought together as one to enable individuation. The process includes a meticulous routine of dream work, active imagination, and shadow work. All this is needed on top of complex and advanced academic study. The emphasis on personal inner work reflects Jung's own approach to his life and his therapeutic model and sets Jungian analysts aside from other therapists and psychologists.

Jungian analysts work with clients, called analysands, first helping them to bolster their Ego, making them strong for their journey into the unconscious, and then helping them uncover their shadows and complexes and where they originated from. Analysts can act as guides to the unconscious realm, as all have done the work exploring it themselves and continue to do so. Jung held that, due to the constant development and evolution of psyche through our lifetime, integration of our conscious and unconscious demands constant, lifelong work. Jungian

Fig. 15 *Mandala Golden Flower,* by one of Jung's analysands

analysts should be actively involved in their own inner work at the same time as guiding analysands in theirs.

All Jung's ideas and methods are incorporated into his therapeutic framework, including word association, dream analysis, shadow work and active imagination. Jung often asked his analysands to create mandalas during therapy.

The Mandala

A mandala is a sacred, circular, geometric design made up of intricate, detailed patterns of images and symbols, joined together in a single, central point. The repeating geometric patterns and light flames lead out from the centre point, representing the inner most part of Self.

The word 'mandala' means 'circle' in Sanskrit, the classical language of India, in Hinduism, Buddhism and Jainism, and it is often used to help focus and enlighten the mind in prayer and meditation. In Eastern traditions, the mandala represents the spiritual journey, starting from outside to the inner core, through layers of transformation. Jung viewed the mandala as, 'the psychological expression of the totality of the self' (1960). He believed they were an archetypal representation of the pattern of order:

> *'[A] psychological view – finger marked with a cross, or circle divided into four, superimposed on the psychic chaos so that each content falls into place and the weltering confusion is held together by a protective circle'* (1964).

As such, mandalas could be used in life and in therapy to help bring the mind into order and the different components of the psyche together for healing and transformation.

Jungian analysis is not about providing the answers or telling people what to do, but helping them to explore their own psyche, discover their true purpose in life and reach individuation. As we have seen, Jungian inner work can be a deeply healing, but also perilous journey. It involves exploring unseen realms of the unconscious. Just as we would consult a map and a guide to help us explore a new terrain in our physical, outer world, Jungian analysts can help us safely and effectively navigate the inner world of our psyche. Among

Fig. 16 A mandala, typical of those inspired by Carl Jung. The repeating geometric patterns and light flames lead out from the centre point, representing the inner most part of Self.

Jung's suggested methods for inner work are practices we can all use in our everyday lives: in dream interpretation, in shadow work, and in active imagination.

Dream Interpretation

Throughout this book, we have seen how important dreams are to Jung in his own inner work and individuation, and in developing his theories. Jung and Freud shared a fascination and many a discussion and debate on dreams and their function. Freud believes our dreams to represent repressed, mainly sexual, urges. Jung sees them as much more: a means of portal to our unconscious, a means of communication through the symbolic language of the archetypes. Repressed thoughts and ideas from our personal unconscious, our shadow, archetypes from our collective unconscious, as well as our anima or animus, all populate our dreams as our unconscious mind tries to permeate and influence our consciousness. For Jung, our dreams can also function as precognition, showing us what may be to come. For example, he believed that his terrifying dreams of blood, death and destruction in 1913 and 1914 related to the build-up and outbreak of World War I. Jung experienced a recurrent vision of a monstrous flood rising up, leaving behind a rubble of civilization. He saw the drowned bodies of thousands of people and the whole sea turned to blood. In other dreams, he saw barren and frozen lands. He experienced the last dream of this kind in June 1914 shortly before war broke out on 28 July.

Jung came to believe his dreams foreshadowed World War I. This was one of the most turbulent times of his life and his dreams may also have represented the changes and challenges in his mind as he was breaking from the constraints of Freud's psychology and the death of old ideas that no longer fitted with his theories. His dreams may have reflected the path the world was taking into war or the new path he was taking in his life and work.

Jung believed dream analysis to be one of the most important paths to self-understanding, 'because dreams are the most common and most normal expression of the unconscious psyche, they provide the bulk of the material for its investigation' (Jung, 1961). Recording, analyzing and reflecting on our dreams is essential for us to be able to understand ourselves. Jung, who claimed to analyze around 2,000 dreams a year, believes that dream analysis provides the foundation for all other forms of inner work. It is the key to our unconscious mind, enabling us to see what is there, what we need to heal, and what we need to make better use of. Jung believes that each image within a dream contains symbolic representation of things we have repressed in our personal unconscious, of the archetypes of our collective unconscious. Each image can have many symbolic interpretations, influenced by our cultural framework and personal experiences.

In looking for meaning in a dream we may first amplify its images, looking to images in religion, myths and fairy tales. Jung warns that amplifying symbols out of the context contained within the dream could close our mind to its real and full meaning. We should always look at the dream as a whole and the role and interaction of symbols within it. Jung also stresses the importance of looking at a dream in relation to the dreamer's own life and what it means in that context. Symbols should also be interpreted in relation to dream series

– dreams that happen over time – in a similar way that referring to an earlier episode in a TV series makes sense of something confusing in the latest one.

A single dream can carry meaning on three different levels. First, it can be understood on a literal, objective level: for example, you dream about your schoolteacher and take that as literally being a dream about them. Second, dreams can be subjective whereby the meaning represents something else personal within you. The schoolteacher could represent a need to exert more, or less, authority over a situation you are in. Third, dreams can also be archetypal in meaning, bringing a message from the collective unconscious into your world. The teacher could represent the mentor in the Spirit archetype.

Dreams can be understood as the place our conscious mind goes to when we are unconscious. When we have no control over our awareness, it can freely explore the contents of our mind, including the shadows we hide from ourselves. Dreams are the response of the unconscious to what is going on in our mind. Jung believes them to play an important healing function by compensating for things we are conscious of doing or thinking that are wrong. Dreams show where our mind has become imbalanced; they indicate what we need to pay more attention to.

Self-development and individuation demand constant communication between the conscious and unconscious. Dreams provide that opportunity, thus facilitating our growth. The more we engage with, study and learn from our dreams, the greater and faster will be our evolution in life.

Fig. 17 *The Dream in the Orchard* by Bill Lewis.

Shadow Work

We discussed Jung's concept of the shadow self in Chapter 3. Here we turn our attention to how these shadows can be integrated into our psyche through shadow work, enabling us to learn their lessons and transform, to achieve individuation. Jung explains:

> *'Everyone carries a shadow, and the less it is embodied in the individual's conscious life, the blacker and denser it is. If an inferiority is conscious, one always has a chance to correct it. Furthermore, it is constantly in contact with other interests, so that it is continually subjected to modifications. But if it is repressed and isolated from consciousness, it never gets corrected.'* (1938)

The aim of shadow work is not to eliminate our shadow but to recognize it as an integral part of our psyche and integrate it into our consciousness. For example, take someone who has a shadow causing an inferiority complex. They may project this onto anyone who is assertive and self-confident, seeing them as arrogant and selfish. This can lead them to go through life feeling second best and allowing themselves to be pushed around by others with more confidence, which in turn causes resentment that makes them feel guilty, further feeding their shadow. Shadow work would enable them to recognize and name this shadow, trace it back to its origins, discover the experience which led to their low sense of self-esteem and work to rebuild this. Analysis and inner work will help them feel more able to assert themselves in the world, opening up their choices and opportunities and diminishing their resentment. This enhances positive experiences of themselves, their life and their relationships.

All of us have shadows and they are all different and unique to us. The first stage in shadow integration, or shadow work, is recognizing our shadow and what we are hiding there. The best way to see our shadows is to pay careful attention to things that trigger strong reactions. This is where your shadow manifests itself. People and situations that cause instant, negative feelings, dislikes and behaviours show where your shadow is being projected. Noting recurrent themes in all of these people and situations will show you the nature of your shadow.

Once we have identified our shadows, we can discover where they came from and the lessons they hold for our integration of the psyche. Dream analysis and active imagination are useful methods for this. Shadow work is never easy. It necessitates us looking into the darkest areas of our psyche at the things that are most uncomfortable for us to examine. While we can address some of our shadows alone, many of us carry deep-set shadows that are best addressed with the help of an analyst or therapist. For example, shadows often emerge as addictions. This often involves a complex mesh of shadows and complexes that are best worked on within a clinical setting. Jung is keen to remind us that, as well as addictions to substances and gambling, shadows can be expressed in addictions to belief systems, philosophies and stereotypical and prejudicial ideas, such as through 'isms' like sexism or racism.

Shadow work means looking honestly at our regrets and failings and making sure we learn from them and do not make the same mistakes again and again. It involves exploring our past, our childhood, our family patterns to see where these originate. Where lessons can be learned, we must learn them. Some shadows simply need us to acknowledge them. We don't always have to like these aspects of ourselves, but we must accept them and welcome them into our psyche.

Active Imagination

In Jungian psychology, active imagination invites and enables a dialogue between the conscious and unconscious, bridging the gap that separates them. By doing so we are consciously opening our awareness to the unconscious, allowing it to fantasize while maintaining active attention of what it is showing us. It involves us switching off the business of our conscious mind with all the noise of work, social media, politics, current affairs, the lives of our family and friends etc., and tuning in and listening to our inner voice. Like in dreams, this often speaks to us through a symbolic language.

Jung believes that active listening enables all aspects of our psyche to move through our consciousness and express themselves. Our job is to hold them in our awareness long enough to glean understanding from them. To enable this, Jung suggests we write down what emerges in a journal, or draw or paint what we see and experience. During Jung's 'creative illness' and experiments with his unconscious, he painted pictures and mandalas daily to explore the state of his psyche and what was happening in there. Many of these can be seen in Jung's account of his journeys with active imagination in The Red Book. He believed artistic creation to be one of the most effective ways of engaging and expressing his relationship with his inner world. He made many drawings, paintings, wood and stone carvings and works of creative writing during the process of active imagination. Writing and expressing our fantasies and daydreams is another effective means of expression.

Active imagination demands us to be open minded and not critical. To listen to the images deep within us, we must allow them to move through our minds and express themselves, then allow a 'free association' – a chain of related ideas, images or words – to build in our consciousness. This can reveal our shadow and complexes, our associations of ideas, thoughts and attitudes around archetypes.

However, it is important to view active imagination as a dialogue between our conscious and unconscious mind. Like all conversations, if our conscious mind takes over, disagrees with what it sees, rejects what it sees, judges and censors, then our unconscious can no longer express itself. All relationships have their tensions and the relationship between our conscious and unconscious in active imagination is no different. Jung believes that recognizing and holding that tension, learning about it and expressing it, can bring deep healing and the wholeness we need to achieve our individuation.

However, Jung expresses the need for caution when working with active imagination. We need to remember that his own journey led him into a 'creative illness' and near breakdown. Active listening carries the danger of flooding and overwhelming our awareness or leading us to spend so much time in our unconsciousness that we lose touch with reality. As such, it is a process that should be used under the guidance of Jungian analysts or other trained psychological professionals.

Conclusion

Jung's pioneering work opened new horizons for the study of the human mind that crossed rational, scientific psychology and psychiatry into the world of art, literature, myth, spirituality and religion. His ideas are at the core of modern psychological theory and research in areas such as personality, the unconscious and evolutionary psychology.

Therapy and Self-Development

Jung's work on schizophrenia was fundamental in understanding some of the underlying psychological processes in thinking, mood and behaviour. His theories and therapeutic ideas underpinned developments in mental health research and practice, many of which remain relevant to this day. Jungian analysis, the progression of inner work on the persona, shadow and anima/animus, is practised all over the world in the treatment of depression, trauma, addiction and other mental health disturbance.

Qualifying as a Jungian therapist necessitates a large investment in time and money, with a requirement of personal analysis at least three times a week for a minimum of four years, alongside an intensive training course. This makes Jungian analysis and therapy an expensive option, especially as it involves commitment to a lengthy process. This can be a significant barrier for potential therapists and analysands alike. Jungian theories are often blended with other therapeutic approaches, such as cognitive behavioural therapy (CBT) and counselling, in integrated therapies. Jung's ideas have also inspired art and creative therapies.

As we have seen, Jung used mandala art in his personal analysis and with many of his clients. He also enjoyed playing with stones on the shore of Lake Zürich and studying the structures and symbols that emerged. The idea of spontaneous play, for all ages, is central to creative therapies. It enables patterns, images and symbols to surface from our unconsciousness for us to explore for meanings and associations.

In one of his most famous and influential books, *Modern Man in Search of a Soul* (1933), Jung stresses the importance of our acknowledging soul and spiritual connections. Without this, we will struggle to find our purpose and meaning in the world. Jung perceives lack of 'spirit' or human 'soul' to be causing a sickness at the heart of Western life in the 20th century, leaving us with no compass with which to navigate chaos, uncertainty and trauma.

Many believe we have carried the malaise from our lack of spirit and soul into the 21st century. Jung's ideas on spirituality and the esoteric, alongside the collective unconscious and individuation, have gained popularity as more of us have tuned into the idea that there is more to life. Many of us believe that we are connected to each other and to some 'source'; that we have a purpose to fulfil in our lives. Books, to help us achieve self-growth and transformation in order to understand and become our 'highest self', our most 'authentic self' or 'best self', are constantly among the bestsellers, and many are based on Jungian ideas and processes, including shadow work, dream analysis and active imagination.

Archetypes and the Esoteric – Astrology and Tarot

Jung was an avid follower of astrology in his own life and pioneered the use of astrological charts in diagnosis and therapy. He believed astrology to be a universal, cosmic form of patterns and dynamics between planets and signs representing archetypal images. The planets represent the mythological gods, themselves archetypal manifestations, and the zodiac signs represent archetypal characteristics and symbology. Throughout time, people have turned to astrology during periods of uncertainty. With the recent global pandemic and deep fears about our environment and the very future of our planet, we are living in hugely tentative and changeable times and astrology has become hugely popular, with signs and symbols appearing more and more across fashion, art and social media. According to Jung, astrology provides us with an invaluable, symbolic insight into the workings of the human mind and can act as a map and guide to our purpose and individuation.

Tarot is another esoteric, or mystic practice that has grown in popularity in recent years. The cards were once associated mainly with fairground fortune telling or foreboding messages in spooky movies. It is now seen as a useful tool in self-development and life coaching. This would be no surprise to Jung who believed the cards to be, 'descended from the archetypes of transformation,' (1959). The images on the cards relate to the 12 archetypal images identified by Jung. Looking at these can help us access these archetypes in our unconscious mind and explore our relationship with them to enable self-development, healing and growth. Jung also mentioned the Chakra system, yoga and I Ching as alchemic structures and processes (1959). All these practices have gained popularity in our modern search for meaning and transformation.

The Arts

Jung's work remains a great inspiration for many across the arts. His ideas on the symbolic representation of archetypes are hugely influential in visual art, especially in understanding how abstract art, with no apparent obvious meaning, can evoke similar responses and emotional reactions among its viewers. The inner of the psyche, especially the unconscious and the process of individuation are also popular themes for Jungian-inspired artists.

In 1949, the mythologist, Joseph Campbell (1904–1987), published his description of the 'hero's journey', the common structure of the journey taken by the archetypal hero of the world of myth and story. Campbell depicted the protagonist's quest through life, whereby he is challenged and helped by the archetypes, grapples with his shadow and, ultimately, reaches his destiny and individuation. This Jungian framework is the backbone to many of our best-loved stories, novels and films. George Lucas used Jung and Campbell's framework when creating the structure and themes of his Star Wars canon. Many of Lucas' characters are instantly recognizable as archetypal images, such as Luke, the hero; Leia, the damsel in distress who comes to represent the mother; Han Solo, the trickster and Yoda the spirit. Confronting the shadow is a popular motif in a story, a good example being Frodo's battle with the dark and selfish side of himself brought out by wearing 'the ring' for too long in Tolkien's The Lord of the Rings trilogy.

Synchronicity is also used as many a plot development. The 1998 film Sliding Doors, written and directed by Peter Howitt, follows two contrasting storylines showing how the life of Helen, the central character, would have played out following a synchronistic moment of just catching or just missing a London tube train. Since then, the term 'sliding-doors moment' has been given to one of those portentous moments when we recognize that a meaningful coincidence, a moment of synchronicity, has changed our direction in life.

The English rock band, The Beatles, were inspired by Jung's works during their psychedelic stage and interest in Eastern religion during the 1960s and they included his portrait on the cover of their 1967 album Sergeant Pepper's Lonely Hearts Club Band. For Jung, man needs a spiritual side, as spiritual understanding is an important part of the human psyche that needs to be addressed and integrated within the process of individuation. He makes a differentiation between religion and spirituality, opposing the control and restriction imposed by organized religion and seeing it as a potential cause of shadows when we fail to meet prescribed standards. Jung sees spirituality 'as real as hunger and the fear of death [...] as basic, as profound, as essential as these other deep guides or archetypal patterns' (1933).

Jung was a great traveller who voyaged into the unknown realms of the psyche and unconscious and returned to show us how to understand ourselves and our purpose in the world. His theories are deep and all encompassing, and we have only touched the surface of his main ideas in this book. Jung's central idea is that we need to discover our self, know our self, accept all of our self, discover our purpose and become whole. He writes, 'The privilege of a lifetime is to become who you truly are' (1963).

Through his painstaking inner work and exploration, C.G. Jung certainly achieved this and gifted us with the ideas and methods to do the same.

Bibliography

Works by Jung

Jung, C. G. (1919) *Studies in word-association; experiments in the diagnosis of psychopathological conditions carried out at the Psychiatric clinic of the University of Zurich, under the direction of C. G. Jung* . New York: Moffat, Yard & Co.

Jung, C.G. (1921) T*he Collected Works, Vol 6: Psychology Types.* Routledge & Kegan Paul, (this edition 1971).

Jung, C.G. (1933) *Modern Man in Search of a Soul,* Routledge & Kegan Paul.

Jung, C.G. (1953) T*he Collected Works, Vol 12: Psychology and Alchemy.* Routledge & Kegan Paul.

Jung, C.G. (1953) *Four Archetypes.* Zurich, Bollingen Foundation.

Jung, C.G. (1954) *The Collected Works, Vol 17: The Development of Personality.* Routledge & Kegan Paul.

Jung, C.G. (1955) *Synchronicity.* London: Ark.

Jung, C.G. (1957) *The Collected Works, Vol 1: Psychiatric Studies.* London, Routledge & Kegan Paul.

Jung, C.G. (1958) *The Collected Works, Vol 11: Psychology and Religion East and West.* Routledge & Kegan Paul.

Jung, C.G. (1959) *The Collected Works, Vol 9, Pt 1: The Archetypes and the Collective Unconscious,* London, Routledge & Kegan Paul.

Jung, C.G. (1960) *The Collected Works, Vol 8: The Structure and Dynamics* of the

Psyche. Routledge & Kegan Paul.

Jung, C.G. (1963) *Memories, Dreams, Reflections*. London, Fontana, Collins & Routledge & Kegan Paul (this edition 1995).

Jung, C.G. (1964) T*he Collected Works, Vol 10, Civilisation in Transition*, London, Routledge & Kegan Paul.

Jung, C.G. (1974) *Dreams*. New Jersey, Princetown University Press.

Jung, C.G. (2009) *The Red Book*. Zurich, Philemon Foundation.

Jung, C.G. (2018) *Jung on Astrology* (selected and introduced by Rossi. S. & Le Grice, K.), London, Routledge.

Other works cited

Adler, G & Jaffé, A. (Eds) (1973) *Letters of C.G. Jung, Vol 1 1906–1950*. London, Routledge.

Adler, G & Jaffé, A. (Eds) (1976) *Letters of C.G. Jung, Vol 1 1951–1961*. London, Routledge.

Bishop, P. (1995) *The Dionysian Self. C.G. Jung's Reception of Friedrich Nietzsche*, Berlin and New York, Walter de Gruyter.

Brome, V. (1978) *Jung, Man and Myth*. London, Macmillan.

Campbell, J. (1949) *The Hero with a Thousand Faces*, New York: Pantheon.

C.G. Jung Club Lectures (1975) Interview with Gret Baumann-Jung, 27 February. https://soundcloud.com/cgjungclublectures/an-interview-with-gret-baumann-jung-27021975

Clay, C. (2016) *Labyrinths: Emma Jung, Her Marriage to Carl and the Early Years of Psychoanalysis*. London: Harper Collins.

Ellenberger, H.F. (1970) *The Discovery of the Unconscious. The History and Evolution of Dynamic Psychology*. New York, Basic Books.

Freud, S. (1896). 'The Aetiology of Hysteria'. In Gay, P. (ed). *The Freud Reader*. London: Vintage, 1995.

Freud, S. (1913) *The Interpretation of Dreams*. London, Macmillan. First published in 1899 as *Die Traumdeutung*. Vienna, Franz Deuticke.

Freud, S. (1991) T*he Freud/Jung Letters: The Correspondence Between Sigmund Freud and C.G. Jung*. London, Penguin.

Herbert, W. (2018) 'The concept of the 50-minute hour: Time forming a frame for the unconscious.' *International Forum of Psychoanalysis*, 27(1):1-10.

Huskinson, L. (2004) *Nietzsche and Jung: The Whole Self in the Union of Opposites*. London, Routledge.

Laurens, Van der Post (1975) *Jung and the Story of Our Time*. New York, Pantheon.

Molton, M.D & Sikes, L.A. (2011) *Four Eternal Women*. Thirsk, Fisher King Press.

Schopenhauer, A. (1995) T*he World and Will and Idea*. London, Phoenix. First published in German in 1818.

Wolff, T. (1956) *Structural Forms and the Feminine Psyche*. Zurich, Student Association, C.G. Jung Institute.

Biography

Sarah Milne is a British psychologist, author and journalist who lives in Hastings, on the South Coast of England. Sarah did her PhD at the University of Sheffield's Psychology Department, researching the gap between intention and behaviour. Psychology remains at the heart of her writing, and she remains fascinated by the things that motivate and influence our behaviour. She is an avid people watcher and collector of stories. When she is not writing books or reading them, Sarah enjoys exploring and adventuring with her three grown-up children and Shih Tzu, Freya.

Acknowledgements

I could thank every one of my family and friends for their words of support or a cup of tea or wine when needed during my tie writing this book. Please know how much you are loved and appreciated. Special thanks are certainly due to Alice Bowden, my wonderful editor, for her patience and help in editing and polishing the manuscript. Also to Norrin Radd for inspiring me, encouraging me, and nagging me when needed, to write and keep writing until the book is done. Thank you!

Picture Credits:

Front image: unknown, upload by Adrian Michael, Public domain, via Wikimedia Commons. **Fig. 1**: LOwens at English Wikipedia, CC BY-SA 3.0 <https://creativecommons.org/licenses/by-sa/3.0>, via Wikimedia Commons **Fig 2**: Andreas Schwarzkopf, CC BY-SA 3.0 <https://creativecommons.org/licenses/by-sa/3.0>, via Wikimedia Commons. **Fig 3**: StefanoRR at Italian Wikipedia, Public domain, via Wikimedia Commons. **Fig 4**: Prints & Photographs Division. Library of Congress (123), Public domain, via Wiki-media Commons. **Fig 5**: Unknown author., Public domain, via Wikimedia Commons. **Fig 6**: See page for author, CC BY-SA 4.0 <https://creativecommons.org/licenses/by-sa/4.0>, via Wikimedia Commons. **Fig 7**: Sigmund Freud's 1909 Visit to Clark University, Public domain, via Wikimedia Com-mons. **Fig 9**: Dornicke, CC BY-SA 4.0 <https://creativecommons.org/licenses/by-sa/4.0>, via Wiki-media Commons. **Fig 10**: Rubin Museum of Art, Public domain, via Wikimedia Commons. **Fig 11**: Unknown author, published by the National Printing & Engraving Company, Chicago-Modifications by Papa Lima Whiskey, Public domain, via Wikimedia Commons. **Fig 13**: Maxence, CC BY 2.0 <https://creativecommons.org/licenses/by/2.0>, via Wikimedia Commons. **Fig 14**: Donrpd, CC0, via Wikimedia Commons. **Fig 15**: Mandala made by an unknown patient of Jung's before 1929 (public domain) (https://commons.wikimedia.org/wiki/File:Mandala_Golden_Flower_Jung.JPG), „Mandala Golden Flower Jung",

This exciting new series of books sets out to explore the life and theories of the world's leading intellectuals in a clear and understandable way. The series currently includes:

Philosophy
Who the Hell is Jean Paul Sartre?
Who the Hell is Ludwig Wittgenstein?
Who the Hell is Immanuel Kant?
Who the Hell is Michel Foucault?
Who the Hell is Aristotle?
Who the Hell is Plato?
Who the Hell is David Hume?
Who the Hell is Friedrich Nietzsche?

Psychology
Who the Hell is Sandra Bem?
Who the Hell is Carl Jung?
Who the Hell is Abraham Maslow?
Who the Hell is Jean Piaget?
Who the Hell is Stanley Milgram?
Who the Hell is B.F. Skinner?
Who the Hell is Melanie Klein?

Politics
Who the Hell is Ayn Rand?
Who the Hell is Jean-Jacques Rousseau?
Who the Hell is Karl Marx?
Who the Hell is Betty Friedan?
Who the Hell is Olympe de Gouges?

Art History
Who the Hell is Erwin Panofsky

Sociology
Who the Hell is Jane Jacobs?